LANCASTER

LANCASTER

THE HISTORY OF BRITAIN'S MOST FAMOUS WORLD WAR II BOMBER

CHRISTOPHER CHANT

This is a Parragon Book
First published in 2003

Parragon
Queen Street House
4 Queen Street
Bath BA1 4HE, UK

Copyright © Parragon 2003

ISBN 0-75258-769-2

Editorial and design by
Amber Books Ltd
Bradley's Close
74–77 White Lion Street
London N1 9PF
www.amberbooks.co.uk

A copy of the CIP data for this book is available from the British Library.

Printed in China

CONTENTS

Introduction

The Lancaster heavy bomber produced by the Avro company was one of the finest weapons to enter large-scale production and service with any of the nations involved in World War II. The Lancaster was the primary weapon of the Royal Air Force's chief offensive arm, Bomber Command, in its night offensive against Germany.

Many thousands of air and ground crews remember the Lancaster for the raids on Germany's industrial cities in the years 1943–45. But many also remember it for special operations like the 'Dam Buster' raid against the dams in the Ruhr industrial region, the sinking of the German battleship *Tirpitz*, and the use of 'Tallboy' and 'Grand Slam' penetration bombs against U-boat pens and viaducts carrying canals and railways.

Lancaster VCs

Production of the Lancaster totalled 7,374 aircraft, the vast majority of them with Rolls-Royce Merlin engines. Of the 31 Victoria Crosses awarded to men of the British and Commonwealth air forces, 22 went to men of Bomber Command. Of these 22 awards, ten were made to members of Lancaster air crews while an eleventh was made to Wing Commander Leonard Cheshire for repeated gallantry while flying three types of bomber; the Armstrong Whitworth Whitley and the Handley Page Halifax as well as the Lancaster.

The United Kingdom declared war on Germany on 3 September 1939. Despite the threat of war that had been real at least since the rise to power of Adolf Hitler in 1933, the UK was still very poorly prepared for a modern European war despite strenuous efforts to modernise and enlarge its armed forces.

Heavier bombs, heavier bombers

In this period of steadily deteriorating European stability, the RAF had nonetheless been radically upgraded. By 1939 Bomber Command possessed the means to attack targets in most parts of Germany, although only with very small bomb loads, and plans had been laid for a new generation of heavy bombers altogether superior to anything else planned in Europe.

Moreover, considerably heavier bombs were being developed to equip these new bombers. In 1939 the heaviest bomb in operational use by the RAF was a 454kg (1000lb) weapon, which could be delivered by twin-engined machines like the Whitley, Handley Page Hampden and Vickers Wellington. But the 227kg (500lb) general-purpose bomb was more commonly employed when RAF Bomber Command started to attack German cities in May 1940.

Coastal Command introduced the semi-armour-piercing 907kg (2000lb) bomb in May of the same year, and the weapon was used by Bristol Beaufort twin-engined warplanes to attack German warships.

To produce a bomber

capable of carrying a substantial bombload to targets several hundreds of miles away depended on a combination of factors in the design specification – wing area, fuselage volume, the power of the engines, and fuel capacity. The RAF knew that militarily effective attacks on distant German targets would need large aircraft with either four powerful or two very powerful engines. The first of Bomber Command's four-engined heavy bombers were the Short Stirling and the Handley Page Halifax that first flew in prototype form on 14 May and 25 October 1939 respectively, while the companion twin-engined heavy bomber was the Avro Manchester that made its maiden flight on 25 July 1939. Despite the fact that it was smaller than the Stirling and Halifax, the Manchester was the only one of these three machines that was able to deliver the RAF's newest bomb – the 1814kg (4000lb) 'blockbuster' high-capacity blast bomb. This weapon was designed to descend below a stabilising parachute, and was carried from the spring of 1941 by Wellington bombers.

The only other four-engined heavy bomber whose development had been ordered before World War II was the Supermarine Type 317, originally conceived by the late R.J. Mitchell (designer of the Spitfire) to satisfy the Air Ministry's specification B12/36. Two prototypes were under construction when they were severely damaged in a bombing attack on the

Supermarine works at Itchen on 26 September 1940. With the Stirling already at an advanced stage, the effective loss of these prototypes prompted the Air Ministry to abandon the project so that Supermarine could concentrate its efforts on production and further development of the Spitfire.

Limitations

The Stirling and the Halifax entered service in the second half of 1940. Both the aircraft marked a further increase in Bomber Command's offensive capability on paper, but it was to be nearly another year before either started to make a significant contribution to the British war effort. Both the new bombers had important operational limitations. The Halifax was rather under-powered, and the Stirling could not lift a single bomb larger than 907kg (2000lb) even though its short-range bomb load of 6350kg (14,000lb) of smaller bombs was useful.

With its two potent Rolls-Royce Vulture engines the Manchester was also designed to carry a 6350kg (14,000lb) bomb load, including the new 1814kg (4000lb) 'blockbuster'. Unfortunately for the Manchester and its crews, improvement and production of the Merlin had a higher priority in the period between 1937 and 1939, and the Vulture project had been given lower priority. The result was that the Vulture was notably unreliable when it entered service in 1940. The Manchester stayed in

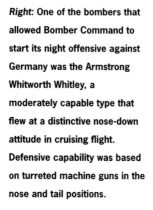

Right: One of the bombers that allowed Bomber Command to start its night offensive against Germany was the Armstrong Whitworth Whitley, a moderately capable type that flew at a distinctive nose-down attitude in cruising flight. Defensive capability was based on turreted machine guns in the nose and tail positions.

Left: Seen in flight over the city of Lincoln, together with a BAe (Avro/Hawker Siddeley) Vulcan delta-winged bomber, is the Lancaster Mk I of the Battle of Britain Memorial Flight.

service with Bomber Command for 18 months but Avro, as a private venture, had started work on a Manchester derivative with the two Vulture engines replaced by four Merlins.

Revised design

Work on this revised design was almost complete even as the Manchester was being evaluated at the Air Ministry's Aircraft and Armament Experimental Establishment. But it was not until after Avro had completed its first 200 Manchester bombers that the company offered the Lancaster to the Air Ministry. The company argued that the Lancaster would have better overall performance and superior payload/range capabilities than the Halifax. It would also be simple to place in production as a result of its close similarity to the Manchester.

The Air Ministry agreed with Avro, and the company completed the Lancaster prototype only four months after they received the contract. From the beginning it was clear that the Lancaster had enormous potential – especially because it could carry significant weights of new and ever larger bombs.

The potential of the Lancaster was soon realized, and the new bomber built up a reputation greater than that of any other British bomber of its period. The new aircraft was rapidly brought into full production, and the manufacturing process eventually involved a total of 1.5 million men and women. Large numbers of companies, both large and small, delivered components and subassemblies to the main centres of production and assembly. The advent of the Lancaster and the other four-engined bombers allowed the phasing out of the Whitley and Hampden from RAF service, and by 1945 Bomber Command had 52 heavy bomber squadrons with 1300 aircraft.

In addition to its reliability and availability in large numbers, the Lancaster was also notable for its versatility. Most important was its adaptability for the carriage of a variety of specialized bombs. These weapons included the 'Tallboy', 'Grand Slam' and 3629kg (8000lb) 'blockbuster' or 'cookie' high-capacity bombs: the Lancaster was the only British bomber able to deliver all three of these weapons.

Below: This head-on view of a Lancaster Mk I reveals the aircraft's basic similarity to the Manchester in its definitive form without the centreline fin but with longer-span outer wing panels carrying an extra pair of engines.

CHAPTER ONE

The Origins of the Lancaster

It was inevitable that the invention of the aeroplane would inspire the military to investigate ways that it could be used for war. World War I propelled the evolution of the bomber from a flimsy, unreliable machine barely capable of crossing the English Channel into a heavy bomber capable of attacking the German capital, Berlin, from bases in eastern England.

Opposite: The Handley Page Hampden, a contemporary of the Whitley and precursor of the Lancaster.

Below: The Royal Naval Air Service was given strategic mobility by the creation of seaplane carriers such as HMS *Ark Royal*, equipped with two steam cranes to lift floatplanes between the deck and the water.

The first primitive bombing raids were flown in the Italo-Turkish War of 1911–12, beginning in November 1911, when Giulio Gavotti dropped three 2kg (4.4lb) grenades from an Etrich Taube monoplane over a Turkish position near Tripoli in Libya.

Trials

The UK was a comparatively late and half-hearted entrant into the field of heavier-than-air military aviation when the Royal Flying Corps, containing Military and Naval Wings, was established in 1912. The first known bombing trials by a British aeroplane were undertaken in March 1912 by aircraft of the Naval Wing, when a number of weighted objects (not actually bombs) were dropped at Eastchurch to investigate the effects of their carriage and release on aircraft performance and handling. In 1913 there followed further trials when a Short seaplane was flown over ground explosions of differing severity to establish the lowest altitude at which an aeroplane might drop its bombs without suffering damage from the explosions on the ground.

In this period the officers of the Military Wing and their superiors in the army continued to believe that the aeroplane would be used mainly for reconnaissance. But those on the naval side felt that there was great scope for more offensive use of the aeroplane for bombing and torpedo bombing. From an early date the Admiralty envisaged using seaplanes to launch torpedoes against enemy ships, with the seaplanes ferried to the operational area by specially converted tenders. It was a Short 'Folder' flown by Squadron Commander A.M. Longmore, at Calshot on 28 July 1914, which launched the first torpedo from a British seaplane.

Floatplanes were produced to carry offensive loads of relatively small bombs (often based on the Royal Navy's standard 152mm/6in shell with fins added) as an alternative to the torpedo. Even the earliest torpedo weighed 367kg (810lb) and later ones were over 454kg (1000lb), burdens which

Above: **Some of the first attempts at strategic bombing were made by the Royal Naval Air Service. Here a Short Type 166 bomber floatplane is being recovered by crane onto HMS** *Ark Royal* **off Mytilene in the Aegean Sea in January 1916.**

posed formidable problems for the aircraft of the time. Although the Royal Navy sponsored a great deal of research into the air-launched torpedo and ordered a large number of aircraft to carry and launch such weapons, only limited use was made of them in World War I. One exception was the Dardanelles campaign of 1915, where they were used effectively.

Bombs at sea

The Naval Wing was separated from the RFC and was brought under the direct control of the Admiralty to become the Royal Naval Air Service in July 1914. The RNAS soon adopted the air-launched bomb as the most versatile weapon against targets at sea or on land. Aircraft designed for the torpedo bombing role were soon converted for the carriage of bombs weighing between 4.5 and 51kg (10 and 112lb). The Royal Navy requisitioned and converted cross-Channel and Isle of Man ferries (the *Empress, Engadine, Riviera, Ben-my-Chree, Manxman* and *Vindex*) as carriers, each equipped for the carriage of three or four sea-

planes. The world's first aircraft (or rather seaplane) carrier built as such was HMS *Ark Royal*, which entered service early in 1915 with provision for up to eight seaplanes.

Isolated bombing raids by aircraft lowered from carriers onto the sea before an operation and then recovered the same way after it were tried against several land targets belonging to the Imperial German navy, culminating in an attack against Cuxhaven on Christmas Day 1914. The raid inflicted no significant damage, but the threat of more such attacks prompted the German navy to shift part of its High Seas Fleet east through the Kiel Canal into the Baltic.

The most capable and celebrated of the RNAS's early leaders was Charles R. Samson. He had been the first commanding officer of the RFC's Naval Wing and, after the start of World War I in August 1914, he took the Eastchurch squadron to Antwerp. From here the squadron flew many harassment raids against the Germans, including an attack on 8 October by Squadron Commander S. Grey and Flight Lieutenant R.L.G. Marix against the Zeppelin sheds at Düsseldorf and Köln. Samson's next posting was to lead the naval squadron of landplanes sent to the Aegean island of Tenedos in March 1915 for operations against the Turks in the Dardanelles campaign. It was one of these aircraft, flown by Samson, which delivered the first 227kg (500lb) bomb – the heaviest in the world at that time.

Strategic bomber

Having initially been equipped and trained for torpedo attacks against German shipping on the high seas, the RNAS soon began to realize that the low numbers of German ships at sea favoured a switch to bombing operations against stationary targets. As these raids showed themselves successful, larger aircraft with better performance and heavier bomb loads were developed, and were manufactured in larger numbers.

Before the end of 1914 the Royal Navy decided that the RNAS should have a genuinely large bomber with the endurance to carry a heavy bomb load for both long-range bombing attacks and long-duration coastal patrols. They opened discussions with Handley Page about the manufacture of such an aircraft. Within one year the company produced a prototype of the Type O/400 heavy bomber, which was the first British strategic bomber to enter service.

Military myopia

But while the RNAS was forging ahead with a heavy bomber capability, under army control the RFC was not exploring the military potential of the aeroplane to anything like the same extent. Younger officers were keen, but were often stymied by the short-sightedness of more senior officers. Evidence of this short-sightedness at work can be seen in the trials held in August 1912 to find the best aeroplane for RFC service. The regulations under which they were held included no requirement for the carriage of an offensive or defensive military load. The winning design, by S.F. Cody, had no development potential and was already technically obsolete.

The Royal Aircraft Factory B.E.2, designed by

Left: **Photographed on an airfield near St Omer in north-eastern France on 18 July 1918, this Royal Aircraft Factory F.E.2b night bomber of No 142 Squadron is being armed for a sortie. The armourer is fusing a 51kg (112lb) bomb under the fuselage, and on the two underwing racks are eight 9.1kg (20lb) Cooper bombs.**

Geoffrey de Havilland, had been denied the chance to compete on equal terms at the trials because it was a government-created machine that might have jeopardized the chances of the aircraft created by private industry. The need to encourage private companies was a central policy of the time, but its effect was to exclude the B.E.2, without doubt the best of all the aircraft seen in the military trials.

Carnage

Nonetheless the B.E.2 was eventually ordered into production, and three years later the B.E.2c variant of this pioneering military aeroplane was the mainstay of British tactical support bombing over the Western Front. In this three-year period the army's refusal to pay serious consideration to the design and procurement of aircraft able to carry gun and/or bomb armament made inevitable the aerial carnage that followed in 1915 when the Germans introduced the world's first true fighters – the Fokker E series of monoplanes.

Even in the face of rapidly increasing aerial losses

to the Fokker fighters, the army's political and service leadership still remained obstinately resistant to the realities of war in the air, and it was mid-1916 before the first genuinely capable British fighters and bombers appeared over the Western Front. This meant that aircraft designed without any provision for armament of any kind, like the B.E.2c and the F.E.2b, were still in widespread service despite their technical obsolescence and the degradation of their performance resulting from the belated addition of armament.

The main weapons of the British bombers from March 1915 to the middle of 1916 were the 4.5, 9.1 and 45.4kg (10, 20 and 100lb) Hales bombs, to which were added 45.4 and 51kg (100 and 112lb) bombs from the Royal Laboratory at Woolwich Arsenal, and a 152.4kg (336lb) fragmentation bomb from the Royal Aircraft Factory. By the end of 1915 there had appeared a number of heavier bombs like the 235.9kg (520lb) light case and 249.5kg (550lb) heavy case weapons, but as yet there were no RFC aircraft able to carry these bombs.

Right: **The best British heavy bomber to see useful service in World War I was the Handley Page 0/400, a development of the pioneering 0/100 with more powerful engines and a number of operational improvements suggested by experience with the 0/100.**

Left: In World War I the aeroplane began to emerge as a potent force in the conduct of land operations. Many single-seat fighters and two-seat general-purpose types were equipped for this role, using their machine guns to strafe soldiers on the ground and 9.1kg (20lb) light bombs such as those shown here to attack machine gun nests and artillery positions.

None of the bombers under development for the RFC entered service until the later months of 1916. The greatest hopes were pinned on the Airco D.H.3 and D.H.4, both designed by de Havilland. By the standards of mid-1915, when work on the type began, the D.H.3 was a very capable aeroplane. But even before the first flight of the prototype the army had cancelled production plans as it believed that the

bombing of German industrial towns was not needed and that the twin-engined bomber was impractical.

Procurement scandal

Procurement problems persisted well into the war, with commercial producers resenting the system's perceived preference for inferior Royal Aircraft Factory machines, and RFC aircrew deeply dissatis-

Below: The first genuinely successful British day bomber was the Airco D.H.4 designed by Geoffrey de Havilland. The bombs in front of the aeroplane second from the left are 104kg (230lb) weapons, of which the D.H.4 could carry two externally.

fied with obsolete and unsuitable aircraft which cost hundreds of their fellows' lives.

The combination of commercial and service unrest eventually broke into the open in parliament. The Government were forced finally to take action. Continued parliamentary pressure eventually brought fairer and more efficient systems for military procurement. From now on the two services would release requirements only after the relevant air arms, commercial manufacturers, and the services' research and design agencies had discussed them. The resulting specification would then be cir-

culated to all manufacturers who could offer a realistic design. Other features of the system included the extension of commercial and national security to all contractors, competitive evaluation by service establishments, and the letting of contracts and subcontracts purely on the basis of efficiency, cost and delivery requirements.

The new system could not be introduced overnight, because the immediate cancellation of existing contracts would have left fighting and training units bereft of aircraft (albeit obsolete aircraft). So for a time the new procurement system continued in parallel with the old. In these circumstances, the new system was bound to take some time to yield results. By the end of 1916 the need for large numbers of aircraft designed specifically as bombers had finally been appreciated by the RFC. In 1917 a large number of specifications for bombers of all types were issued, including heavy bombers that were finally deemed to be feasible through advances in airframe and engine technologies.

The two British aircraft that were most important in proving the significant role that could be played by the bomber were the Type O/100 heavy bomber and the D.H.4 day (or light) bomber. The capabilities of these two machines reflected the thinking of the services that sponsored them. The Royal Navy was concerned with the projection of strategic power over long ranges, while the army (within which the RFC was only a junior corps without a strong voice of its own) was more concerned with the development of tactical weapons that could exert a battlefield influence. It was only after 1 April 1918, when the RFC and RNAS were combined to create the Royal Air Force, the world's first independent air force, that the two concepts fused. The army's and Royal Navy's initial contributions were respectively the D.H.4 and F.E.2b light bombers of the 41st Wing, and the Type O/100 heavy bombers of No 1 Squadron.

Considerable progress was made with the development of the bomber force in the period up to the Armistice in November 1918 that ended World War I. By this time the British could field some 49 bomber squadrons (though six of these had only a secondary bombing capability). Of these, four were based in the UK, 37 in Belgium and France, eight in Italy and the Balkans, and one in Mesopotamia. As well as larger numbers of improved aircraft, these

Above: **The standard heavy bomber of the Royal Air Force in the early 1920s was the Vickers Vimy, a comparatively small but effective twin-engined type that could carry two 112kg (230lb) and eight 51kg (112lb) bombs internally and externally.**

Right: The Boulton Paul Overstrand was a development of the same company's Sidestrand for the medium day bomber role.

Below: A British attempt to reduce the cost of developing and procuring separate types of heavy aircraft saw the emergence of machines designed to operate in the bomber and transport roles. One such type, which progressed no further than a single prototype first flown in 1932, was the four-engined Gloster T.C.33.

squadrons could also call on better bombs. Whereas the heaviest bomb in service at the beginning of 1917 had been the 249.5kg (550lb) heavy case weapon, which only the Type O/100 could carry, by November 1918 Type O/400 bombers were dropping the 748.4kg (1650lb) SN bomb on targets in Germany. The still newer Type V/1500 was being readied for service with the 1520kg (3350lb) SN Major bomb that, but for the armistice, would have been carried from bases in Norfolk to Berlin.

Treasury cuts

The implementation of the Armistice meant that these strategic raids on the enemy's capital never happened, but in the years that followed imaginations ran wild: what were the real capabilities of the strategic bomber? General Sir Hugh Trenchard was now Chief of the Air Staff, and as such commanded the largest and most capable air force in the world. At this time these were large numbers of aircraft on order under many contracts, but the Treasury summarily cancelled 92% of them, throwing many workers into unemployment and devastating the British aircraft manufacturing industry.

In November 1918 the Air Ministry listed the aircraft that were already in service and would be retained for the RAF. They also set out the aircraft designs that had already been ordered in prototype form and would be evaluated in competitions to find the successors to existing service types. Of the bombers, the Airco D.H.9A was only just entering service and was to remain a standard type for several years, but some production contracts were cancelled, and no plans were made for a replacement in the immediate future.

The standard medium bomber, another new Airco product, was the D.H.10 Amiens. Only limited production had already been planned, so a replacement was scheduled for 1920–21 with prototype contracts already placed for the Boulton & Paul Bourges, Sopwith Cobham, Avro Type 533 Manchester, Airco D.H.11 Oxford and Airco D.H.14 Okapi.

The standard heavy bombers – the two-engined Type O/400 that was already in service and the four-engined Type V/1500 on the verge of full service – might have been thought to be of deterrent value in the uncertain world that had supposedly entered a period of peace after the 'war to end all wars'. But the existing force of Type O/400s was deemed sufficient

for the few bomber squadrons that were not to be disbanded, and the Type V/1500 was cancelled. The only other modern British bomber in existence was the Vickers Vimy. This was in no way an exceptional machine, but it was reliable and was destined to remain in service into the later 1920s as a dual-role bomber and transport aeroplane.

RAF cutbacks

Despite the international tensions following the end of the war, the British Government, strapped for cash, trimmed the RAF to a stump that only just retained the capability for survival and later expan-

Above: **The nose turret of the Boulton Paul Overstrand was powered pneumatically and carried a manually elevated machine gun. This turret did not in itself constitute any advance in firepower over those it replaced, but it provided the gunner with a more comfortable environment and paved the way for more advanced turrets.**

Right: **The Handley Page Heyford was an extraordinary night bomber produced essentially as an interim type.**

sion. Within two years of the end of World War I, the strength of the RAF in terms of personnel, aircraft and bases was cut back by between 80 and 90 per cent, leaving wholly insufficient strength for the operational tasks it might have to shoulder for a country with global responsibilities.

Trenchard had assumed that the independence of the RAF was inviolate, but soon discovered that the army and Royal Navy did not agree and wanted to divide the RAF between them. In these circumstances Trenchard sought a role that the RAF could undertake more effectively and cheaply than either of the other two services, and in doing so helped to secure the future of his service. This role derived from the collapse and dissolution of the Ottoman Empire, and the establishment of new French and British mandated territories in the Middle East.

Imperial policing

Extending north to south between the Caspian Sea and the Arabian Sea, and west to east between the Mediterranean littoral and the western frontier of Persia, this vast area was largely desert with great mountainous regions, and was populated in many parts by tribal peoples, many of them nomadic. For some years the army had tried unsuccessfully to limit the warlike activities of tribal groups, but was always rendered powerless by the size of the area and the mobility of the groups they were trying to check.

Trenchard proposed a novel concept of 'imperial policing' using aircraft like the D.H.9A for both mobility and, when needed, firepower. The system worked remarkably well right from its beginning, one light bomber squadron achieving the results that had proved impossible for larger ground forces, and at lower cost.

The concept of 'imperial policing' was expanded steadily. Before long the larger types of British aircraft, initially the Vimy and then a succession of twin-engined machines that could double as troop transports and bombers, were shifting small bodies of troops between trouble spots all over the mandated territories, at a speed that negated the mobility of the warlike tribesmen.

Ten-year rule

Back in the UK, politicians had enunciated the 'ten-year rule', largely to provide a pretext to avoid the

Left: **The Armstrong Whitworth A.W.29 prototype was an attempt to create an advanced two-seat light bomber. Of all-metal construction with retractable main landing gear units, the A.W.29 had a dorsal turret armed with a single machine gun, and cells in the wing for the carriage of four 113kg (250lb) bombs.**

need for expensive and unpopular technical improvement and enlargement of the armed forces. The rule fixed the concept that the UK would not become involved in another major war without a ten-year period of increasing tension that would provide adequate time for the implementation of diplomatic moves to defuse the situation or, failing those moves, for the armed forces to be expanded and re-equipped. As events were to show, the ten-year rule might have been workable, but only if the correct diplomatic moves were backed by adequate armed strength.

Yet the emergence of the ten-year rule actually benefited Trenchard and the Air Ministry. Trenchard was a firm believer in the concept of strategic bombing. He saw this as the RAF's primary reason for existence, with all other operational roles subordinated to

it. And the heavy bomber was the core of the strategic bombing concept – a potent offensive weapon able to destroy an enemy's industrial capability and social fabric, and thus his ability to wage a sustained war. Within the context of the ten-year rule Trenchard felt his task was to preserve only the nucleus of a strategic bombing capability, with squadrons that could provide a seed for later expansion, and at the same time to push the bomber to the front of technological capability through the ordering of a stream of steadily improving prototypes

Below: **Created to meet a requirement for a heavy night bomber that could double as a transport, the Handley Page H.P.43 prototype appeared in 1932.**

Above: The prototype of the Handley Page Hampden, which first took to the air on 21 June 1936, is seen here with the makeshift nose and dorsal fairings that were initially fitted.

Right: The Vickers Wellington was the best medium bomber available to the Royal Air Force on the outbreak of World War II. These are Wellington Mk III aircraft with two-gun nose turrets and four-gun tail turrets.

from commercial manufacturers, which would be kept in existence by a steady number of small contracts for the best types to emerge from the prototype process.

Accordingly, the 1920s saw the design of a variety of new bomber types, many of which reached the prototype evaluation stage but few of which entered squadron service. The most successful in terms of length of service and numbers manufactured, were the Vickers Virginia heavy and Hawker Hart light bombers. These were still in first-line service into the mid- and late-1930s respectively, yet neither type was significantly different in oper-

ational concept from the Type O/400 and D.H.9A of World War I.

Change at the top

At the start of January 1930 Air Chief Marshal Sir John Salmond succeeded Marshal of the Royal Air Force Lord Trenchard as Chief of the Air Staff. Trenchard had been a 'bomber man', and was now followed by an officer who, although not a confirmed 'fighter man', had commanded the RAF's home fighter force, then known as the Air Defence of Great Britain, between 1925 and 1929. Salmond decided that his first priority had to be the

improvement of the UK's ability to defend itself in the air, for he believed the British fighters then in service were closer to their ancestors of World War I than was the case with the bombers.

The great world economic depression which had started in 1929 was already well under way when Salmond took over the reins of the RAF, and he knew sacrifices might have to be made on the bomber side if the fighter capability of the RAF were to be improved. Salmond was fortunate in that a new and highly capable light day bomber, the Hawker Hart, was on the verge of entering service. While the Virginia and two Handley Page types, the Hyderabad and Hinaidi, were clearly obsolete, the last two years of Trenchard's leadership had seen the issue of several important heavy bomber requirements for which a number of prototypes were being developed.

More duds

The first of the two heavy bomber requirements was embodied in specification B19/27. This drew responses from Vickers, Fairey, Handley Page, Hawker, Avro and Bristol. The second of the requirements was carried in specification B22/27 for a still larger heavy bomber, and elicited responses from Boulton & Paul and de Havilland. In the event, specifications B19/27 and B22/27 both failed to produce a genuinely effective modern heavy bomber. The latter was abandoned

when neither of the two three-engined prototypes was successful, while the former resulted in orders for two indifferent twin-engined types, the Handley Page Heyford and the Fairey Hendon.

The Heyford was a biplane with its fuselage attached to the underside of the upper wing, leaving the thickened centre section of the lower wing for bomb stowage, and in addition to poor performance had a number of teething problems that delayed its entry into service. The Hendon was a low-wing cantilever monoplane with a thick-section wing, distinctly limited bomb load and mediocre performance, and took so long to get into service that it was wholly obsolete by the time this happened in November 1936.

As it was clear as early as 1932 that neither the Heyford nor the Hendon would have any long-term potential, the Air Ministry issued a new specification for what was officially described as a heavy bomber for nocturnal operations but was in fact little more than a medium bomber. Specification B9/32 led to the Handley Page Hampden and the Vickers Wellington. In the previous eight years the flight performance of the British heavy bomber had improved by about ten per cent, largely as a result of the introduction of more powerful engines, but the new specification called for considerably higher performance, and made it inevitable that the RAF would turn to a new generation of monoplane bombers.

Left: Another interim type to allow the introduction of the monoplane concept to the Royal Air Force's bomber arm, the Handley Page Harrow was a dual-role bomber and transport.

CHAPTER TWO

The Manchester

The clean lines and devastating bomb load of the Lancaster were inherited from an earlier RAF bomber, the two-engined Avro Manchester. The Manchester was powered by the Rolls-Royce Vulture engine, an unreliable and technically complex powerplant which led to the loss of many aircrew during the early years of World War II.

By 1936 the British authorities were becoming increasingly alarmed at the pace of German rearmament, and could no longer ignore the use to which the military expansion was being put in support of German territorial claims. The result was an acceleration and expansion of the UK's own rearmament programme. An early result of this process was the issue early in 1936 of specification B12/36. This called for a four-engined strategic bomber that could be designed, developed and placed in production with the utmost speed, and yet provide Bomber Command with a high-speed means to deliver a sizeable weapons load over considerable range. The crew was to comprise six men, the defensive armament was to include multi-gun nose, ventral and tail turrets, and the bomb bay was to be designed to carry 227kg (500lb) general-purpose bombs or 907kg (2000lb) armour-piercing bombs. The maximum take-off weight was stipulated at 21,773kg (48,000lb), although a growth figure of 24,041kg (53,000lb) was allowed and a long-term figure of 29,484kg (65,000lb) envisaged.

The specification also demanded rapid design, development and manufacture through the use of well-proved structures, viceless handling characteristics so that the bomber could be operated effectively by the newly trained crews of the expanded RAF, and dimensions to permit the new aircraft to fit into existing hangars. For the benefit of the specification these were deemed to have a maximum clear opening of only 30.48m (100ft)

Above: Seen in front of some of their Manchester bombers are personnel of No 106 Squadron, including the unit's commander, Squadron Leader Guy Penrose Gibson (centre front).

Opposite: A Manchester Mk IA in the markings of Bomber Command's No 207 Squadron.

even though many hangars in fact had an opening of 38.40m (126ft).

Stirling

The first result of this specification was the Short Stirling, which was the first four-engined heavy bomber to enter service with the RAF's Bomber Command. The Stirling was also the only British bomber to enter service after having been designed for four-engines from the outset – the later Avro Lancaster and Handley Page Halifax were both four-engined developments of designs originally planned for two engines. The Stirling was a work-

SHORT STIRLING MK I

Type: heavy bomber

Crew: pilot and co-pilot side by side on the enclosed flight deck, and navigator/bombardier, radio operator, flight engineer/gunner and two gunners carried in the fuselage

Armament (defensive): two 7.7mm (0.303in) Browning trainable forward-firing machine guns with 1000 rounds per gun in the power-operated Frazer-Nash FN5 nose turret, two 7.7mm (0.303in) Browning trainable machine guns with 1000 rounds per gun in the power-operated Frazer-Nash FN5 ventral turret, and four 7.7mm (0.303in) Browning trainable rearward-firing machine guns with 1000 rounds per gun in the power-operated Frazer-Nash F.N.20A tail turret

Armament (offensive): up to 6350kg (14,000lb) of bombs or other weapons carried in a lower-fuselage bomb bay rated at 6350kg (14,000lb) and in six wing cells each rated at 227kg (500lb), and generally comprising seven 907kg (2000lb) bombs carried in the fuselage or 21 227kg (500lb) bombs carried in the fuselage and wing

Powerplant: four Bristol Hercules XVI air-cooled radial piston engines each rated at 1230kW (1650hp) for take-off and 783kW (1050hp) at 3125m (10,250ft)

Fuel: internal 10,246.7 litres (2706.9 US gal; 2,254 Imp gal) plus provision for 1000.1 litres (264.2 US gal; 220 Imp gal) of auxiliary fuel in tanks installed in the wing bomb cells; external none

Wing: span 30.20m (99ft 1in); aspect ratio 6.72; area 135.63 sq m (1460 sq ft)

Fuselage and tail: Length 26.59m (87ft 3in); height 6.93m (22ft 9in)

Weights: empty 21,274kg (46,900lb); normal take-off 26,944kg (59,400lb); maximum take-off 30,845kg (68,000lb) later increased to 31,752kg (70,000lb)

Performance: maximum speed 'clean' 418 km/h (226kt; 260 mph); at 3200m (10,500ft); cruising speed, economical 346km/h (187kt; 215 mph) at 4570m (15,000ft); initial climb rate not available; climb to 3660m (12,000ft) 42 minutes 0 seconds with maximum bomb load; service ceiling not available; typical range 3750km (2023nm; 2330 miles) with a 680kg (1500lb) bomb load declining to 1191km (643nm; 740 miles) with a 6350kg (14,000lb) bomb load.

Below: **The first four-engined heavy bomber to enter British service in World War II was the Short Stirling.**

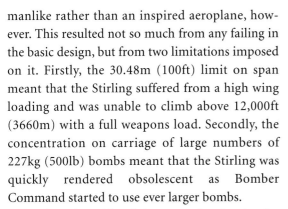

Left: The need to give the Stirling a larger angle of attack at take-off without increasing the wing's incidence led the Short design team to adopt long main landing gear legs. Here armourers are preparing to load parachute-stabilized mines into a Stirling's weapons bay.

manlike rather than an inspired aeroplane, however. This resulted not so much from any failing in the basic design, but from two limitations imposed on it. Firstly, the 30.48m (100ft) limit on span meant that the Stirling suffered from a high wing loading and was unable to climb above 12,000ft (3660m) with a full weapons load. Secondly, the concentration on carriage of large numbers of 227kg (500lb) bombs meant that the Stirling was quickly rendered obsolescent as Bomber Command started to use ever larger bombs.

On the other side of the operational coin, the Stirling was monumentally sturdy and could return to base even after suffering very heavy damage. It was also, in general, a tractable aircraft to fly – except during take-off and landing, in which its characteristics can be described only as unforgiving.

Clipped wings

The Air Ministry received design submissions from Armstrong Whitworth, Short and Supermarine, and ordered prototypes of the Short and Supermarine types. Short initially proposed a design with good high-altitude performance provided by a wing spanning 34.14m (112ft), based on the Sunderland maritime reconnaissance flying boat. But to meet the specification the Short design team had to revise its concept with a wing of reduced span and greater chord, the resulting decrease in aspect ratio inevitably reducing high-altitude capability.

The Air Ministry, faced with steadily more depressing intelligence information about the extent and speed of German rearmament in the later 1930s, agreed to this degradation of capability, ordered two prototypes of this S.29 design and revealed that it would start to order production aircraft even before the prototypes had flown. Short had coped with such a challenge when under pressure by Imperial Airways to deliver the flying boats of the 'C' or 'Empire' class as rapidly as possible, but the new bomber was the first large landplane it had produced since the Scylla and Syrinx of 1934, and was also its first aeroplane with retractable landing gear.

When it was planning the 'Empire' class, Short had found it useful to test the aerodynamics and controllability of the new type with the Scion Senior small-scale aerodynamic prototype. The same process was followed with the new bomber, for which the S.31 was designed as the half-scale prototype with four 67.1kW (90hp) Pobjoy Niagara III radial engines. The S.31 made its first flight on 19 September 1938 and revealed good handling characteristics, much to the satisfaction of Short. As a result of its test flying of this aeroplane, however, the RAF requested greater wing incidence. Short had selected an incidence of 3º for the best possible cruise performance, but the RAF

was more concerned with improved take-off performance and asked for the incidence angle to be increased to 6.5°. This would have required a major and time-consuming revision of the central fuselage, so the compromise reached was a considerable lengthening of the main landing gear legs to given a higher ground angle. This change was tested on the S.31 from the end of 1938, when the aeroplane was also revised with four 85.7kW (115hp) Niagara IV engines.

Crash-landing

Construction of the two S.29 prototypes continued in the early part of 1939, and the first of them made its maiden flight on 14 May 1939, only to be written off as it landed: one of the brakes had seized, and the asymmetric strain caused one of the main landing gear units to break. The landing gear was redesigned, and the second prototype made a successful first flight on 3 December 1939. Production was already under way, and the first Stirling Mk I bomber made its initial flight in May 1940.

The first production aircraft were of the Stirling Mk I Series 1 type with four 1025kW (1375hp) Bristol Hercules II radial engines; next came the Stirling Mk I Series 2 with four Hercules XI engines in Short-designed nacelles that were simpler to manufacture; and finally there appeared the definitive

Right: The Stirling, seen here in the form of the fourth production aeroplane, marked an interim stage in the development of the defensive armament of British heavy bombers.

Stirling Mk I Series 3 with Hercules XI engines in Bristol-designed nacelles. The defensive armament comprised two 7.7mm (0.303in) Browning machine guns in the power-operated nose turret, four 7.7mm machine guns in the power-operated Boulton Paul (Frazer-Nash) F.N.20A tail turret, and two 7.7mm guns in the power-operated and retractable ventral turret. This last caused considerable unhappiness among crews: it tended to inch down during take-off, and when extended for combat caused considerable performance-degrading drag. The turret was generally removed, therefore, and replaced by four 0.303in lateral-firing machine guns in two beam positions. When an improved turret became available in the form of the power-operated F.N.7 unit with two 7.7mm trainable machine guns, this was installed in a new dorsal position.

Delivery of the Stirling Mk I began in August 1940, and deliveries of this initial model totalled 756 aircraft from Short at Rochester in Kent, Short & Harland at Belfast in Northern Ireland, a 'shadow factory' run by Austin Motors at

Below: This Stirling served with No 199 Squadron in the electronic countermeasures and Bomber Command support roles between the middle of 1943 and the end of World War II.

29

HANDLEY PAGE HALIFAX MK I

Type: heavy bomber

Crew: pilot on the enclosed flight deck, and bombardier/gunner, navigator, radio operator, flight engineer and two gunners carried in the fuselage

Armament (defensive): two 7.7mm (0.303in) Browning trainable forward-firing machine guns in the power-operated Boulton Paul Type C nose turret, four 7.7mm (0.303in) trainable machine guns with 1160 rounds per gun in the power-operated Boulton Paul Type E tail turret, and one 7.7mm (0.303in) Vickers 'K' trainable lateral-firing machine gun in each of the two manually-operated beam positions

Armament (offensive): up to 6577kg (14,500lb) of bombs or other weapons carried in a lower-fuselage bomb bay rated at 5897kg (13,000lb) and in six wing cells each rated at 227kg (500lb), and generally comprising one 3629kg (8000lb) bomb, or two 1814kg (4000lb) bombs, or four 907kg (2000lb) bombs, or two 907kg (2000lb) and six 454kg (1000lb) bombs, or eight 454kg (1000lb) bombs, or two 680kg (1500lb) mines and six 227kg (500lb) bombs, or nine 227kg (500lb) bombs carried in the bomb bay, and six 227 or 113kg (500 or 250lb) bombs carried in the wing cells

Powerplant: four Rolls-Royce Merlin X liquid-cooled Vee piston engines each rated at 854kW (1145hp) for take-off

Fuel: internal 8210 litres (2168.9 US gal; 1806 Imp gal) plus provision for 482.8 litres (127.5 US gal; 106 Imp gal) of long-range fuel in two 681.9 or 436.4 litre (180.1 or 115.3 US gal; 150 or 96 Imp gal) tanks in the outermost bomb cells in the wing, and for 3864.1 litres (1020.8 US gal; 850 Imp gal) of ferry fuel in three weapons-bay and two fuselage tanks; external none

Wing: span 30.07m (98ft 8in); aspect ratio 7.81; area 116.125 sq m (1250 sq ft)

Fuselage and tail: length 21.74m (71ft 4in); height 6.32m (20ft 9in); wheel track 7.52m (24ft 8in)

Weights: empty 16,330kg (36,000lb); maximum take-off 27,216kg (60,000lb)

Performance: maximum speed 'clean' 450.5km/h (243kt; 280mph) at 5075m (16,500ft); cruising speed not available; initial climb rate not available; service ceiling 5820m (19,100ft); typical range 4828km (2605nm; 3000 miles) with a 1361kg (3000lb) bomb load declining to 1706km (920.5nm; 1060 miles) with a 3629kg (8000lb) bomb load

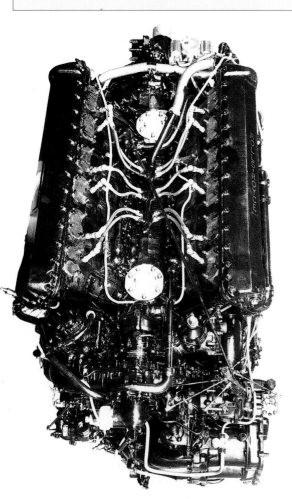

Longbridge in Birmingham, and a 'shadow factory' run by Roots Securities at Stoke-on-Trent: these four sites assembled all the aircraft, although they received assemblies and components from another 20 factories in the mainland UK and Northern Ireland. The first service aircraft were delivered to No 7 Squadron, and after training the Stirling Mk I entered operational service in February 1941. Aircraft in service at the end of 1942 received the revised designation Stirling B.Mk I.

Halifax

The next four-engined bomber to enter RAF service was the Handley Page H.P.57 Halifax. Although eventually overshadowed by the Avro Lancaster, the Halifax was still a magnificent warplane that deserves greater attention than it has generally received. The early Halifax bombers were not quite as 'right' as the early Lancasters, and it took considerable effort and time to eliminate all the initial problems. The Halifax matured as an exceptional bomber that in its late-war variants was faster than the Lancaster and could carry a roughly equivalent weapon load even though it was not as fuel economical and lacked the

Lancaster's rate of climb and agility.

The origins of the Halifax can be traced to the Air Ministry's B1/35 requirement for a twin-engined bomber to succeed the Vickers Wellington. The Handley Page design team, under the supervision of George Volkert, planned the H.P.55 as a mid-wing type with two Bristol Hercules radial or Rolls-Royce Merlin Vee engines, and the Air Ministry ordered a single prototype in October 1935. Then came the P13/36 requirement for a somewhat faster medium bomber, and the company decided to recast the H.P.55 as the H.P.56 with the wing reduced in span from 28.96m (95ft) to 27.43m (90ft) and two engines. The company suggested to the Air Ministry that the development of the H.P.56 should be undertaken in two stages, the first with two Hercules engines and the second with the considerably more potent arrangement of two Rolls-Royce Vulture X-

Below: **The Halifax reached its definitive form as a bomber in the Mk III form, as seen in this example of a Halifax Mk III photographed in February 1944.**

type engines. But given the pace and scope of the German rearmament programme the Air Ministry wanted to proceed as rapidly as possible and in April 1937 placed a contract for two H.P.56 prototypes each with two Vulture engines.

Vulture trouble

The aircraft was designed with an all-metal structure and a defensive armament of two 7.7mm (0.303in) Browning forward-firing machine guns in a power-operated Boulton Paul nose turret, four 7.7mm rearward-firing machine guns in a power-operated Boulton Paul tail turret, and one 7.7mm Vickers 'K' lateral-firing machine gun in each of the two manually-operated beam positions. In theory the H.P.56 offered the promise of an excellent warplane, but in practice Handley Page became increasingly concerned about the Vulture engine, which was proving very troublesome in development. The company therefore approached the Air Ministry with the suggestion that the H.P.56 be revised as the H.P.57 with a longer-span wing carrying four Merlin engines. The Air Ministry gave its approval for the change in September 1937, and the H.P.57 began to take shape with a wing enlarged in span to 20.12m (98ft 10in) and carrying outer

Right: **L7277 was the second production example of the Manchester Mk I, and featured the original short-span tailplane with comparatively small endplate vertical surfaces complemented by a centreline fin.**

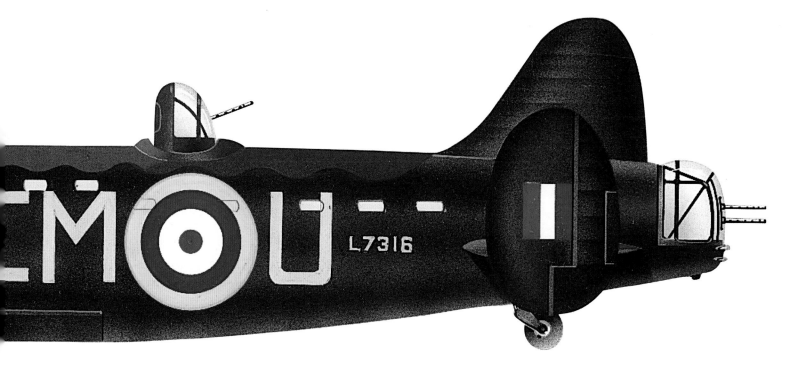

panels still fitted with large Handley Page automatic leading-edge slats but tapered on both the leading and trailing edges rather than on just the leading edge as had been the case with the H.P.56.

Work on the completion of the first prototype was pushed ahead as rapidly as possible, and this machine made its maiden flight on 25 October 1939 (less than two months after the outbreak of World

Above: **Shown in the camouflage scheme applied to aircraft of No 207 Squadron early in 1942, this Manchester Mk I has the two-gun dorsal turret added in January of that year. The aeroplane was lost over Essen on 31 August 1941.**

AVRO MANCHESTER MK IA

Type: medium bomber

Crew: pilot and co-pilot on the enclosed flight deck, and navigator/bombardier, radio operator and three gunners carried in the fuselage

Armament (defensive): two 7.7mm (0.303in) Browning trainable forward-firing machine guns with 1000 rounds per gun in the power-operated Frazer-Nash F.N.5 nose turret, two 7.7mm (0.303in) trainable machine guns with 1000 rounds per gun in the power-operated Frazer-Nash FN21A ventral turret (later replaced by the power-operated Frazer-Nash F.N.7 dorsal turret), and four 7.7mm (0.303in) trainable rearward-firing machine guns with 1000 rounds per gun in the power-operated Frazer-Nash F.N.20 tail turret

Armament (offensive): up to a theoretical 6350kg (14,000lb) but practical 4695kg (10,350lb) of bombs or other weapons carried in a lower-fuselage bomb bay rated at 6350kg (14,000lb), and generally comprising eight 454kg (1000lb) bombs, or four 907kg (2000lb) bombs, or two 1814kg (4000lb) bombs

Powerplant: two Rolls-Royce Vulture I liquid-cooled X-type piston engines each rated at 1312kW (1,760hp) for take-off and 1376 kW (1,845 hp) at 1525m (5,000ft)

Fuel: internal 5273.4 litres (1393.1 US gal; 1160 Imp gal); external none

Wing: span 27.46m (90ft 1in); aspect ratio 7.14; area 105.63 sq m (1137 sq ft)

Fuselage and tail: length 21.14m (69ft 4.25in); height 5.94m (19ft 6in); tailplane span 8.53m (28ft 0in) in early aircraft increasing to 10.06m (33 ft) in later aircraft; wheel track 7.24 m (23ft 9in)

Weights: empty 13,350kg (29,432lb); maximum take-off 25,402kg (56,000lb) standard and 27,103kg (59,750lb) overload

Performance: maximum speed 'clean' 426 km/h (230kt; 265 mph) at 5180m (17,000ft); cruising speed 298 km/h (161kt; 185 mph) at 4570m (15,000ft); initial climb rate not available; service ceiling 5850m (19,200ft); typical range 2623km (1,416nm; 1,630 miles) with a 3674kg (8100lb) bomb load declining to 1931km (1,042nm; 1,200 miles) with a 4695kg (10,350lb) bomb load

War II), powered by four Merlin IX engines each driving a three-blade propeller of the constant-speed type. The second prototype followed on 17 August 1940 with the same powerplant driving different Rotol propellers with densified wood blades, and this machine also had full armament but no leading-edge slats.

The Air Ministry ordered the H.P.57 into production late in 1938 and allocated the name Halifax early in the following year. Production of the aircraft on a very large scale was envisaged, with initial models coming from the English Electric line that was currently delivering the Handley Page Hampden medium bomber, later supplemented by deliveries from an industrial grouping that eventually included the Rootes Group, the Fairey Aviation Co. Ltd. and the London Aircraft Production Group. The Halifax Mk I entered service in November 1940 as the huge industrial machine began to gather production pace, and the first squadron to receive the

Below: **This Manchester Mk IA has the definitive pattern of rear fuselage and tail unit, with a wider-span horizontal surface and larger endplate vertical surfaces, that were also adopted for the Lancaster.**

aircraft was No 35 Squadron, which flew its first operation in March 1941. Eventually 64 RAF Bomber Command squadrons flew Halifaxes.

The Halifax was successful from the beginning, although some problems began to emerge with the landing gear retraction system, the reduction gears of the Merlin X engines, and a lateral stability at high weights. These problems were eventually ironed out – in the middle and latter cases by the use of four-bladed propellers in some aircraft, and the later enlargement of the vertical tail surfaces respectively.

Deliveries of the Halifax Mk I totalled 84 aircraft in three subvariants. The Halifax Mk I Series 1 had four Merlin X engines and was stressed for a maximum take-off weight of 26,309kg (58,000lb). The Halifax Mk I Series 2 had four Merlin X engines and was stressed for a maximum take-off weight of 27,216kg (60,000lb), and the Halifax Mk I Series 3 had four Merlin X or Merlin XX engines supplied

with fuel from an increased internal capacity but had the same maximum take-off weight as the series 2 aircraft. Further development of the Halifax, with Merlin as well as Hercules engines, then proceeded in parallel with those of the Manchester and Lancaster. Total production was 6,176 aircraft.

Specification P13/36

The Air Ministry probably never developed any specification with so much attention to detail or as the result of so much consultation before it issued specification P13/36 in November 1936. A major feature of the new bomber was that it should be a medium dive-bomber able to deliver its attack in a 30° dive so that it would have to remain over the target area for only the shortest possible time. The other primary elements of the specification included the ability to operate anywhere in the world, the possibility of alternative payload/range capabilities without modification of the airframe, fuel tankage or bomb bay, a high cruising speed to reduce the time the aeroplane would have to spend over enemy territory, the provision of all-round defence through the incorporation of power-operated nose and tail turrets and also a member of the crew to direct defensive fire, and the ability to operate in the alternative role of a troop carrier with only modest factory modification.

Catapult

In terms of offensive armament, the Air Ministry specification demanded the ability to lift a weapons load of at least 3629kg (8000lb) including two 457mm (18in) torpedoes as an alternative to bombs, as well as the fuel for a range of 3219km (1737nm; 2000 miles) or more at a cruising speed of 442.5 km/h (239kt; 275 mph) at an altitude of 4570m (15,000ft). Provision was also to be included for launch at maximum take-off weight with the assistance of a ground catapult system then under investigation by the Royal Aircraft Establishment at Farnborough. The specification was for two Rolls-Royce Vulture X engines which, the manufacturer estimated, would deliver 1267.5kW (1700hp) for take-off.

Six companies responded to the specification, and of the competing design submissions the HP56 and Avro Type 679 were ordered in prototype form for first flights by January 1939. Handley Page later secured a relaxation of some aspects of the specification, most notably the removal of the ability to carry torpedoes, and then received permission to recast its design as the H.P.57 with four Merlin engines, as the Halifax. At Avro however, Roy Chadwick decided to meet the requirements of specification P13/36 in every respect and, in providing a large bomb bay able to accept the 457mm (18 in) torpedo's length of 5.56m (18ft 3in), paved the way for one of the eventual Lancaster's most important features, namely the ability to carry very large weapons.

The Vulture engine around which the H.P.56 and Type 679 designs had been evolved was essentially two Rolls-Royce Peregrine Vee engines mounted on a common crankcase to create an X-type engine developing about double the power available from current versions of the Merlin engine. As work on the new bomber prototypes proceeded, it became clear that there would be insufficient engines for production of both bombers and along with the technical problems with the Vulture this influenced the decision to terminate work on the H.P.56 in its twin-engined form, and switch that project to the four-engined version that eventually became the Halifax.

Left: L7246 was the first
prototype of the Manchester,
and was completed without
turreted armament for a first
flight from Ringway on 25 July
1939.

Enter the Manchester

This left the field clear for Avro to proceed with the Type 679, and in 1938 the Air Ministry announced a major production programme for a bomber whose performance estimates suggested a maximum weapons load of 5443kg (12,000lb) lifted at a maximum take-off weight of 17,136kg (37,777lb), a maximum speed of 531 km/h (287kt; 330 mph) at 4570m (15,000 ft), and the ability to deliver a 3629kg (8000lb) bomb load over a range of 3219km (1737nm; 2000 miles) at a speed of 465 km/h (251kt; 289 mph) on a basis of a wing that spanned only 21.95m (72ft) with an area of 86.38 sq m (930.00 sq ft).

The Type 679 was of stressed-skin light alloy construction with flush-riveted skinning. The structural heart of the aeroplane was the semi-monocoque fuselage of basically rectangular section with rounded corners to reduce drag. The forward cabin, with bullet-proof glazing and heating air from the coolant radiators in the wing leading edges, accommodated the flight crew of

Below: This rear view of L7246 emphasizes the basic layout of the wing with a flat centre section of constant thickness and chord carrying dihedralled outer panels that were tapered in thickness and chord to their rounded tips.

Above: **This August 1939 side view of L7246, the first prototype of the Manchester, highlights the fact that there was something 'not quite right' about the tail unit.**

pilot and fire controller on the port side. The navigator was seated further aft at his chart table on the starboard side, and the radio operator at the rear near the astrodome used by the navigator for celestial navigation purposes on long-range flights. The other members of the crew were the three gunners for the Nash and Thompson (later Frazer-Nash) F.N.5 nose, F.N.21A ventral and F.N.4A tail turrets, which each carried two 7.7mm (0.303in) Browning machine guns. The fuselage was completed by the large ventral bomb bay, with close-fitting doors.

The first of the two Type 679 prototypes made its maiden flight on 25 July 1939, and trials soon revealed that the aircraft's directional stability was inadequate. This resulted in the addition of a fixed fin like that of a shark above the fuselage. The second prototype made its maiden flight on 26 May 1940, and resembled the revised first prototype in most features except its completion with full defensive armament. Later changes were the replacement of the ventral turret by a Frazer-Nash F.N.7 dorsal turret, the substitution of a wider-

chord central fin for the original shark's fin unit, the replacement of the metal-skinned elevators and ailerons by fabric-covered units, and the extension of span from the already increased figure of 25.04m (82ft 2in) with an area of 98.24 sq m (1057.50 sq ft) to the definitive 27.46m (90ft 1in) as a means of reducing the wing loading and thus improving altitude performance, which fell considerably below the anticipated service ceiling of 7390m (24,250 ft).

A contract for 200 production aircraft had already been placed, and work on these machines began in July 1939. These aircraft switched to a four-gun F.N.20 tail turret, and while the first 20 aircraft were delivered with the same type of tail unit as the second prototype and a maximum take-off weight of 22,680kg (50,000lb), subsequent machines were delivered in the improved Manchester Mk IA standard with a revised tail unit incorporating a longer-span tailplane carrying larger vertical surfaces so that there was no longer any need for the central fin. In this configuration maximum take-off weight increased to 25,447kg

(56,100lb) and then, after the notional maximum bomb load had been boosted to 6350kg (14,000lb) – although 4695kg (10,350lb) was the heaviest load that was ever carried – to an overload figure of 27,103kg (59,750lb).

High loss rate

The Manchester entered service with No 207 Squadron in November 1940, and made its first operational sortie in February 1941. Pilots liked the aeroplane's good handling qualities in the air, but soon discovered that these were more than offset by the great unreliability of the Vulture engine, which was also reluctant to deliver its rated power and also prone to in-flight fires. With only two engines and an unreliable engine type in a highly loaded aeroplane, the Manchester could not maintain altitude on one engine alone, and many aircraft were lost as a result of a single engine failure. Even so, the Manchester equipped Nos 49, 50, 61, 83, 97, 106, 207 and 420 Squadrons of RAF Bomber Command.

There were plans to create a Manchester Mk II with either two Napier Sabre H-type engines each rated at 1566kW (2100hp) or two Bristol Centaurus radial engines each rated at 1879kW (2520 hp), and either of these powerplants could have turned the Manchester into an excellent bomber. Neither type proceeded past the project stage, however, because the adoption of the four-engined Merlin configuration was turning the unsuccessful Manchester into the truly great Lancaster (originally designed Manchester Mk III) and all further development of the Manchester was halted. Production totalled just 200 aircraft, and the aircraft was withdrawn after making its last operational sortie in June 1942.

The Manchester flew 1269 sorties, and suffered the very high loss rate of 40% on operations and 25% on training flights.

Below: **L7288 was the 13th Manchester Mk I off the production line, and was delivered to No 207 Squadron, in whose marking it is seen here. The aeroplane later passed successively to Nos 97 and 61 Squadrons before ending in the hands of No 1654 Conversion Flight at RAF Waddington in May 1943.**

CHAPTER THREE

Development and Production

The most successful and celebrated heavy bomber used by Bomber Command for its night offensive in the second half of World War II, 7300 Lancasters were built over the course of the war – but the design did not begin life until the war was already three months old.

At that time the Avro company's most important design team, under the supervision of Roy Chadwick, was concerned mostly with the development of the Type 679 Manchester twin-engined bomber. Despite the problems with the Vulture engine, the Air Ministry valued the Manchester design for its heavy bomb load and other performance characteristics.

Revised design

Chadwick and his design team still had severe reservations about the long-term viability of the Vulture powerplant, and therefore initiated several studies for versions of the Manchester with a different powerplant. At the end of 1939 Avro were told by the Air Ministry to proceed with the detailed design of the Manchester Mk II that would be a minimum-change development of the Manchester Mk I with two Napier Sabre H-type or Bristol Centaurus radial engines. But this project was soon overtaken by that for the Manchester Mk III with four Merlin engines. Despite the change from two to four engines, the Manchester Mk III was seen as a relatively straightforward development that would retain the Manchester Mk I's fuselage, tail unit and flat wing centre section. This section of the wing had a constant chord and carried the nacelles that supported the retractable landing gear. These nacelles would now be adapted for the Merlin engine in place of the original

Vulture. Beyond the original engine nacelles a new extra section, dihedralled, tapered in thickness and chord, would support the nacelles for the other pair of Merlin engines.

Avro gave the new company designation Type 683 to the revised design, and estimated that it would be able to carry a bomb load of 5443kg (12,000lb) over a range of 1609km (868nm; 1000 miles) at a speed of 394 km/h (212kt; 245 mph) after take-off at a

Opposite: **Bomber Command's Lancasters were rarely as polished as this beautifully maintained and preserved example.**

Below: **A member of No 44 Conversion Flight's ground staff ensures that all is well with the port main wheel of a Lancaster Mk I before take-off.**

two prototypes moved ahead rapidly, and the first prototype made its maiden flight on 9 January 1941. Even to a casual glance the new aircraft was clearly a derivative of the Manchester Mk I, with its original type of short-span tailplane carrying small endplate vertical surfaces supplemented by a centreline surface, and with a similar configuration of defensive armament.

After initial flight trials, the first prototype was delivered to the Aircraft & Armament Experimental Establishment at Boscombe Down for official trials. The second prototype was completed for a maiden flight on 13 May 1941, with the tailplane increased in span from 6.71m (22ft) to 10.06m (33ft) and carrying larger endplate vertical surfaces that removed the need for the centreline fin. The defensive armament of the first prototype was upgraded to the planned production standard, namely two 7.7mm (0.303in) Browning forward-firing machine guns in a power-operated F.N.5 nose turret, four 0.303in rearward-firing machine guns in a power-operated F.N.20 tail turret, two 0.303in machine guns in the power-operated F.N.50 dorsal turret, and two 7.7mm (0.303in) machine guns in the power-operated Frazer-Nash F.N.64 ventral turret.

The prototypes had four Merlin XX engines each rated at 954kW (1280hp) for take-off, 1089kW (1460hp) at 1905m (6250ft) and 1070kW (1435hp) at 3355m (11,000ft), driving a three-blade de Havilland metal propeller of the constant-speed type. The prototype trials were so successful that the Air Ministry decided to terminate Manchester production immediately, after the delivery of only 200

maximum weight of 25,878kg (57,000lb). This estimate suggested that the Type 683 would provide considerably greater capability than the Manchester, even though it would place an additional burden on Merlin production. The Air Ministry thought that the Type 683 would be slightly less capable than the rival H.P.57, but ordered Avro to put the model in production as soon as it had completed its order for 300 Manchester bombers.

As the new model made extensive use of existing components and assemblies, the completion of detailed design work and the construction of the

aircraft, so that construction of the new Lancaster could begin as soon as possible.

Operational trials

The first Lancaster Mk I off the production line flew on 31 October 1941, and on Christmas Eve of 1941 three aircraft were delivered to No 44 Squadron for operational trials. The first operational sorties took place on 10–11 March 1942. Deliveries to operational squadrons were not as rapid as had been hoped, because it proved necessary to strengthen the wing tips and make a number of other changes, including a revision of the upper skinning of the wing, but in general the Lancaster Mk I was very similar to the second prototype.

Operations soon revealed that the ventral turret saw little use and squadrons therefore often removed it. Two officially-inspired changes were the addition of a carefully shaped fairing round the lower edge of the dorsal turret to improve the airflow (it also served to create a taboo track to prevent the gunner firing into any part of the airframe, most especially the vertical tail surfaces); and an increase in internal fuel capacity from 7773.7 litres (2053.6 US gal; 1710 Imp gal) in four wing tanks to 9792.1 litres (2586.8 US gal; 2154 Imp gal) in enlarged standard tanks and additional tanks installed further outboard in the wings.

Immediate success

The Lancaster Mk I was an immediate operational success, as is reflected in the fact that large-scale

Above: **Armourers fit the tail units to general-purpose bombs and prepare to move the bomb train out of the bunkers to the waiting aircraft.**

production saw the delivery of only three more variants (one major and two minor). The Lancaster Mk I remained in production right up to the end of hostilities. But this is not to say that there were not considerable developments during the course of each variant's production run. To give just one example, the bomb bay of the Lancaster Mk I was soon provided with a strengthened support structure for the carriage of a single 3629kg (8000lb) bomb, and then fitted with modified doors to permit the carriage of a single 5443kg (12,000lb) bomb.

The introduction of more powerful engines brought major enhancements of operational capability. With the Merlin XX engine rated at 954kW (1280hp) for take-off with a boost of 0.83 bar (12 lb/sq in) and 1103.5kW (1480hp) at 1830m (6000ft), the Lancaster Mk I had a maximum take-off weight of 27,896kg (61,500lb) and its performance gave a maximum speed of 462 km/h (249kt; 287 mph) at 3505m (11,500ft), a service ceiling of 7470m (24,500ft) and a range of 2671.5km (1441.5nm; 1660 miles) at a cruising speed of 338 km/h (182.5kt; 210 mph) with a 6350kg (14,000lb) bomb load.

The Merlin XX was then replaced by the Merlin 22 with the boost of 0.83 bar (12 lb/sq in) usable for climb as well as take-off. This permitted a maximum take-off weight of 28,577kg (63,000lb) and gave an operational performance that included a maximum speed of 434 km/h (234.5kt; 270 mph) at 5790m (19,000ft) and a range of 3943km (2127.5nm; 2450 miles) with a 2495kg (5500lb) bomb load declining to 1641.5km (886nm; 1020 miles) with a 6350kg (14,000lb) bomb load.

Finally, the introduction of the Merlin 24, rated at 1208kW (1620hp) with a boost of 1.245 bar (18 lb/sq in) for take-off and climb, allowed the further increase in maximum take-off weight to 30,845kg (68,000lb) standard or 32,659 kg (72,000lb) overload.

Further improvements introduced to the Lancaster Mk I included the H2S navigation and bombing radar introduced in August 1943, easily distinguishable by the large opaque Perspex fairing over its ventral antenna: this was a two-edged weapon, however, for while it allowed Bomber Command crews to navigate and bomb more accurately, its emissions could easily be detected by the Naxos receiver that the Germans quickly created

and introduced on their fighters as a means of finding and homing in on H2S-equipped bombers. Another enhancement was the conversion to carry the 9979kg (22,000lb) 'Grand Slam' transonic penetration bomb in 33 Lancaster B.Mk I aircraft with Merlin 24 engines. The bomb doors were removed to accept the bulk of the weapon under the aircraft, and the nose and dorsal turrets, to save weight.

Production expands

Toward the end of 1941 production of the Lancaster Mk I was accelerating so rapidly that there were fears that airframe production would soon outstrip Merlin availability, and so the authorities considered using an engine that was in lesser demand. The choice fell on the Bristol Hercules VI radial engine, rated at 1286kW (1725hp). The Air Ministry ordered two prototypes of this Lancaster Mk II: the second was not completed, and the first made its maiden flight on 26 November 1941 with a slight lengthening of the

bomb bay and the F.N.64 ventral turret.

Trials revealed that the Lancaster Mk II was closely similar to the Lancaster Mk I in performance, with the exception that the service ceiling was only slightly more than 4570m (15,000ft). Even so, it was decided to place the model in pro-

Above: **A trio of Lancaster Mk I bombers of No 44 Squadron, based at RAF Waddington in Lincolnshire.**

Left: **Mechanics of the Royal Air Force work on the two starboard Merlin engines of a Lancaster.**

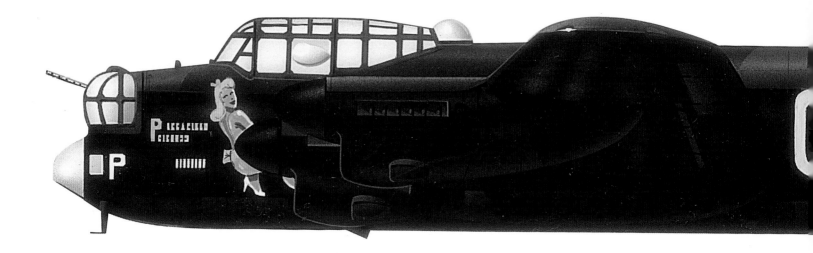

Below: The 5443kg (12,000lb) 'Tallboy' deep-penetration bomb was the second most massive single weapon carried by the Lancaster after the 9979kg (22,000lb) 'Grand Slam'.

duction, and Armstrong Whitworth delivered 300 from September 1942. Some of the later aircraft had the bulged bomb bay introduced on later Lancaster Mk I aircraft, and four Hercules XVI engines rated identically to the original Hercules VI engines. The model was soon redesignated as the Lancaster B.Mk II, but fewer aircraft were manufactured than had originally been expected, because Merlin production held up better than expected and the surplus of airframes stayed relatively low.

The Lancaster B.Mk III, known at the very beginning of its career as the Lancaster Mk III and in the later stages of its life as the Lancaster B.Mk 3, was the direct equivalent of the Lancaster Mk I, but with engines built under licence in the USA by Packard with the local designation V-1650 in place of the original Merlins. When used in the Lancaster B.Mk III, these engines were the Merlin 28 or 38 equivalent to the Merlin 22, or the Merlin 224 equivalent to the Merlin 24. The first trial installation of American-built engines was made in a Lancaster Mk I conversion that flew in August 1942, and the first production aircraft became available later in the same year.

3434 Lancaster Mk Is were manufactured, and 3030 Lancaster Mk IIIs. The Lancaster Mk III had the same performance data as the Lancaster Mk I (the different designation was employed only to indicate the need to follow modified servicing requirements). When, late in 1942, the Royal Air Force introduced role prefixes to the mark numbers of its aircraft, the Lancaster Mks I and III became the Lancaster B.Mks I and III respectively.

Dam Busters

It was 23 aircraft of the Lancaster Mk III type that were adapted for delivery of the 'bouncing bomb'

AVRO LANCASTER B. MK III

Type: heavy bomber

Crew: pilot and co-pilot side by side on the enclosed flight deck, and navigator/observer, bombardier/gunner, radio operator and two/three gunners carried in the fuselage

Armament (defensive): two 7.7mm (0.303in) Browning trainable forward-firing machine guns with 1000 rounds per gun in the power-operated Frazer-Nash F.N.5 nose turret, two 7.7mm (0.303in) trainable machine guns with 1000 rounds per gun in the power-operated Frazer-Nash F.N.50 dorsal turret, and four 7.7mm (0.303in) trainable rearward-firing machine guns with 2500 rounds per gun in the power-operated Frazer-Nash F.N.20 tail turret

Armament (offensive): up to 6350kg (14,000lb) of bombs or other weapons carried in a lower-fuselage bomb bay rated at 6350kg (14,000lb), and generally comprising one 5448kg (12,000lb) bomb, or one 3629kg (8000lb) and six 227kg (500lb) bombs, or one 1814kg (4000lb), six 454kg (1000lb) and two 113kg (250lb) bombs, or six 907kg (2000lb) and three 113kg (250lb) bombs, or six 681kg (1,500lb) mines, or 14 454kg (1000lb) bombs, often in combination with up to 14 Small Bomb Carriers loaded with 3,400 1.8kg (4lb) incendiary bombs. 'Special' aircraft were equipped to carry one 9979kg (22,000lb) 'Grand Slam' or 5443kg (12,000lb) 'Tallboy' deep-penetration bomb, or one 4309kg (9500lb) 'Upkeep' pre-rotated surface-skimming mine, or one 2490kg (5490lb) 1.14m (45in) or 2404kg (5300lb) 0.965m (38in) Type T Capital Ship Bomb

Powerplant: four Packard (Rolls-Royce) Merlin 28 or 38 liquid-cooled Vee piston engines each rated at 1089kW (1460hp) at 1905m (6250ft) and 1070kW (1435hp) at 3355m (11,000ft); or Merlin 224 liquid-cooled Vee piston engines each rated at 1223kW (1640hp) at 610m (2000ft) and 1118.5kW (1,500hp) at 2895m (9500ft)

Fuel: internal 9792.1 litres (2,586.8 US gal; 2154 Imp gal) plus provision for up to 3636.8 litres (960.75 US gal; 800 Imp gal) of auxiliary fuel in one or two 1818.4 litre (480.4 US gal; 400 Imp gal) bomb bay tanks; external none

Wing: span 31.09m (102ft); aspect ratio 8.00; area 120.77 sq m (1300.00 sq ft)

Fuselage and tail: length 20.98m (68ft 10in) with the tail down and 21.28m (69ft 6in) with the tail up; height 6.19m (20ft 4in) with the tail down and 6.25m (20ft 6in) with the tail up; tailplane span 10.06m (33ft); wheel track 7.24m (23ft 9in)

Weights: empty 18,598kg (41,000lb); normal take-off 30,872kg (68,000lb); maximum take-off 32,659kg (72,000lb)

Performance: maximum speed 'clean' 452 km/h (244kt; 281 mph) at 3355m (11,000 ft) declining to 436 km/h (235kt; 271 mph) at 1905m (6250 ft); cruising speed, maximum 365km/h (197kt; 227 mph) at optimum altitude and economical 348km/h (188kt; 216 mph) at 6095m (20,000ft); initial climb rate not available; climb to 6095m (20,000 ft) in 41 minutes 24 seconds; service ceiling 7460m (24,500 ft); maximum range 4313km (2,327.5nm; 2,680 miles) with a 3175kg (7000lb) bomb load and one auxiliary tank; typical range 1673km (903nm; 1040 miles) with a 4536kg (10,000lb) bomb load

Above: **This Lancaster B.Mk III flew a number of important missions with No 405 (Canadian) Squadron, including sorties to Brunswick, Stuttgart and Laon. The aircraft was posted missing after a raid on Haine-St-Pierre on the night of 8–9 May 1944.**

designed by Dr. Barnes Wallis for the celebrated attack by No 617 Squadron in May 1943 on the Möhne, Eder, Sorpe, Ennepe and Lister dams which controlled water levels in the rivers and canals of the Ruhr industrial region. Another special weapon that could be carried by Lancaster Mk III bombers (and also Lancaster Mk I machines) was the 5443kg (12,000lb) 'Tallboy', another weapon designed by Wallis. This was a highly streamlined bomb designed to reach supersonic speed before impacting, which gave it considerable penetration before detonation. The weapon was used successfully against the battleship *Tirpitz*, deep railway tunnels and similar communications targets, and the concrete roofs of U-boat pens.

Changes made later in the production run included the removal of the F.N.64 ventral turret, the frequent replacement of the F.N.50 turret in the dorsal position by F.N.79 or F.N.150 units, and the general replacement of the F.N.20 turret in the tail position by the F.N.121 or F.N.82, the former with four 7.7mm (0.303in) Browning machine guns and the latter with two 12.7mm (0.5 in) Browning machine guns. The heavier-calibre armament was also used in another turret option, the Rose-Rice

Type R No 2 Mk I, often combined with another development late in the war, the 'Village Inn' Automatic Gun-laying Turret incorporating a radar sight for automatic laying and firing of the turret's guns. Like all other Lancaster variants, the Lancaster B.Mk III was operated solely in the European theatre during World War II.

Far East

As the end of the war drew in sight in the second half of 1944, the Air Staff began to plan the use of the Lancaster in support of British operations against the Japanese in the Far East. In its basic form the Lancaster B.Mk III lacked the range for operations in this theatre, so aircraft delivered in 1945 were completed to the Lancaster B.Mk III (FE) standard with a number of tropicalization features and provision for the installation of a large saddle tank, carrying 5455.2 litres (1441.15 US gal; 1200 Imp gal) of fuel, between the rear of the flight deck and the position of the dorsal turret, which was removed. Like the Lancaster B.Mk I (FE), the Lancaster B.Mk III (FE) saw no operational service before the surrender of Japan following the atomic bombings of Hiroshima and Nagasaki in August 1945.

The Lancaster Mks IV and V were considerably improved versions of the basic airframe that eventually matured after World War II as the Lincoln B.Mks 1 and 2.

Inspired by the Lancaster Mk IV with four 1219kW (1635hp) Merlin 85 engines each driving a four-blade propeller, the Lancaster B.Mk VI was a development of the Lancaster Mk III, with the same powerplant and an airframe that was changed only by the omission of the nose and dorsal turrets. The prototype conversion made its maiden flight in the spring of 1944, and another six aircraft followed. Only four of the aircraft were used operationally by Nos 7 and 635 Squadrons. They were used in the electronic warfare role with radar jamming and 'Window' chaff equipment, and even these were withdrawn in November 1944.

The Lancaster B.Mk VII was a development of the Lancaster Mk III with a Martin dorsal turret; a power-operated unit carrying two 12.7mm (0.5in) Browning machine guns. The Martin turret was installed further forward on the fuselage than the Frazer-Nash turret. 180 of these aircraft were built, but they saw service only after the end of World War II, mostly in the Far East.

The Lancaster B.Mk X designation was given to 430 Lancaster B.Mk IIIs built in Canada by Victory Aircraft and identical in all-important respects to the Lancaster B.Mk III.

In the course of World War II the Lancaster was operated by a total of 61 squadrons, flew some 156,000 sorties and dropped 608,612 tons of bombs. The last production aeroplane was delivered in

February 1946, and although the type remained in service after the war with a total of 14 squadrons (eight based at home and six in the Middle East) the Lincoln soon replaced it in home service. The last Lancaster was retired from British service in February 1954, but the type lingered in French naval air arm service for a while longer.

Above: **An armourer prepares to install one of the four 7.7mm (0.303in) Browning Mk II machine guns in the F.N.20 rear turret of a Lancaster.**

Below: **DG595 was the second prototype of the Lancaster, and first flew on 13 May 1941.**

CHAPTER FOUR

The Lancaster in Service

The first three Lancaster Mk I production aircraft were delivered to RAF Waddington on 24 December 1941, where No 44 Squadron, previously flying the Handley Page Hampden, had been selected as the first unit to convert to the new four-engined bomber.

Opposite: Lancaster Mk I of the Battle of Britain Memorial Flight, demonstrating the size of its bomb bay doors.

Below: A tractor driver gives the thumbs-up to a member of the manufacturer's production team after towing a newly completed Lancaster Mk II, characterized by its Bristol Hercules air-cooled radial engines.

At much the same time, the Aircraft and Armament Experimental Establishment at Boscombe Down launched a series of high-intensity flight trials to find any problems that had not hitherto been discovered, and then to find solutions.

Loose wing tips

No 44 Squadron flew its Lancaster bombers on their first operational sortie on 3 March 1942, when four aircraft laid mines. The first bombing operation followed a week later, when two aircraft attacked a target in Germany. One week and three days later No 97 Squadron, the second unit to receive the aircraft, flew their first Lancaster operation, laying mines off the Frisian Islands. But the Lancasters were then taken off operations for a short time to have their wing tips strengthened, after one of No 97 Squadron's aircraft shed its wing tips in a tight turn and was lost in the sea off the coast of Lincolnshire. Another structural problem emerged in April 1943 when a Lancaster under test at Boscombe Down lost part of the upper skin of its wing and crashed. This necessitated the examination and modification of all the Lancaster bombers that had been completed to date.

From the beginning of its life the Lancaster had included a large bomb bay, but an upgraded bomb support system had to be developed to allow the bomber to carry the 3629kg (8000lb) high-capacity 'blockbuster' or 'cookie' bomb that had not been developed by the time the bomb bay was originally designed. At around the same time the depth of the bomb bay was increased by altering the shape of the doors. This allowed the Lancaster to carry a 5443kg (12,000lb) bomb too.

Production

The Lancaster Mk I was manufactured by five companies:

Right: The manufacture of the Lancaster was a major effort for the British war industry during World War II. These are Lancaster centre-section assemblies under construction at Armstrong Whitworth's Baginton factory during 1944.

Avro (894, of which 840 were assembled and test-flown at Manchester and 54 at Yeadon), Metropolitan-Vickers (944 produced at the company's Mosley Road Works in Manchester but assembled and test-flown by Avro at Woodford with the exception of the last 23, which were assembled by Vickers-Armstrong at Chester), Armstrong Whitworth (911 assembled at Baginton near Coventry and later at Bitteswell near Rugby), Vickers-Armstrong (535, of which 300 were assembled at Castle Bromwich and 235 at Chester), and Austin Motors Ltd (150 built at the Longbridge works in Birmingham). The Lancaster Mk III was manufactured by only three of the companies: Avro (2776; 2,135 at Woodford and 641 at Yeadon), Metropolitan-Vickers (136), and Armstrong Whitworth (118).

Production of the Lancaster Mk II was allocated to Armstrong Whitworth, who manufactured all 300 produced. They were assembled at Baginton from September 1942. Many of the early examples of this variant had the deepened bomb bay introduced on later examples of the Lancaster Mk I and were delivered with the ventral turret, while later examples switched to four Hercules XVI engines. As soon as it became clear that production of the Merlin would be adequate to meet Lancaster air-frame manufacture, the order for another 300 Lancaster Mk II bombers to be produced by Vickers-Armstrongs was amended to cover Lancaster Mk I aircraft.

In 1942 the production rate of the Lancaster was accelerated to a significant degree from a monthly average of 23 in January to 91 in December. The production rate continued to climb through 1943 and in the first three-quarters of 1944, peaking at 250 aircraft per month in the late summer of 1944. Of other British aircraft only the Hawker Hurricane and Supermarine Spitfire were manufactured at a higher rate over their whole production lives, although manufacture of the Halifax four-engined bomber was accomplished at a higher rate than that of the Lancaster up to mid-1943. By that time, however, it was more than clear that the Lancaster was the best available bomber, and the production rate of the Halifax slowed as the design was adapted for a number of other important tasks.

Area bombing

When the Lancaster Mk I entered service with Nos 44 and 97 Squadrons in March 1942, Air Vice Marshal Arthur 'Bomber' Harris had been commander-in-chief of Bomber Command for only a few

Left: Even as work continues on the installation of internal features and equipment, the aircraft reaching the head of the production line are raised by a pair of matched lifts so that the main landing gear units can be fitted.

weeks and the command was changing its offensive philosophy from precision attacks on selected targets to attacks on area targets. Nos 44 and 97 Squadrons belonged to No 5 Group, which had been chosen to be the first Bomber Command group equipped solely with the Lancaster. This task had been completed by the spring of 1943, and by this time the Lancaster was also operational with one squadron of No 1 Group and three squadrons of No 3 Group. The increasing pace of Lancaster production meant that Nos 1 and 3 Groups also became all-Lancaster formations, and by the end of World War II half of the Canadian-manned No 6 Group

was also flying the Lancaster, as were six of the Pathfinder Force's squadrons in No 8 Group. By April 1945 the Lancaster was serving with 57 squadrons: the standard types were the Lancaster Mks I and III, although some of No 6 Group's squadrons were operating the Canadian-built Lancaster Mk X.

The Lancaster Mk II entered operational service early in 1943 with a flight No 61 Squadron in No 5 Group, but first equipped a complete squadron only later in 1943, when No 115 Squadron became operational with the aircraft. Another unit of No 5 Group, No 514 Squadron, also flew the Lancaster

Below: This Lancaster was on the strength of No 619 Squadron, a unit of No 5 Group. LM446 was delivered to the squadron at the end of January 1944, and was lost of the night of 9–10 May of the same year after recording 215 hours in the air.

Right: Throughout its major night campaign against Germany, Bomber Command was led by Air Chief Marshal Sir Arthur Harris, seen here examining reconnaissance images of a target area.

Mk II; and three units from No 6 Group also used them, namely Nos 408, 426 and 432 Squadrons.

Primary weapon

In the period between mid-1942 and May 1945 the Lancaster was the primary weapon in Bomber Command's campaign of attrition against Germany's cities and industrial regions. The importance of the Lancaster is attested by the fact that no fewer than ten awards of the Victoria Cross were made to members of Lancaster crews.

On 5–6 March 1943, when the Lancaster had been in service for one year, Bomber Command began the campaign that became known as the Battle of the Ruhr, in which major conurbations in this region (including Essen, Dortmund, Duisburg, Düsseldorf and Essen) came under increasingly heavy attack. In July 1943 the focus of Bomber Command's efforts was switched further to the north, where Hamburg was very badly damaged, and from November Berlin received no fewer than 16 heavy attacks in five months.

Invasion

In March 1944 Bomber Command was switched from its strategic campaign against Germany's cities and industrial regions to support the forthcoming Allied invasion of northwestern France. This involved attacks on the airfields, radar sites and a whole gamut of communications systems in northern France, Belgium and the Netherlands in the months preceding the D-Day assault landing on 6 June 1944. Thereafter, the bombers attacked in tactical support of the Allied forces fighting eastward – although another key target in this period became the sites from which the Germans were launching their 'V weapons'.

From September 1944 Bomber Command reverted to the strategic bombing campaign, and a change from this time onward was the switch to day as well as night operations as Germany's defensive fighter capability was diminished by attrition (especially of capable pilots) and ever-worsening shortages of fuel. The addition of day attacks to Bomber Command's repertoire proved very successful, and allowed the accurate marking of decisive targets like centres of fuel production, key industrial components, communications and transport to degrade still further Germany's capacity for effective defence against the Allied advances.

Precision raids

In addition to its major part in the strategic bombing campaign, the Lancaster was also involved in a number of small-scale special operations that were well publicized in the Allied media. The first of these operations to become well known took place on 17 April 1942, when Nos 44 and 97 Squadrons each sent six Lancaster Mk I bombers to attack the MAN works at Augsburg, where the company manufactured Diesel engines for use in Germany's U-boat fleet. Seven of the 12 bombers were lost, but the raid was nonetheless important as it showed to the British public that the new bomber provided Bomber Command with the means to strike both hard and deep into Germany's heartland.

The Lancaster was operational with nine squadrons of No 5 Group by October 1942, and all these squadrons were sent on another daylight attack on 17 October. The aircraft attacked the Schneider armament works at Le Creusot in France, and only one of the 93 bombers was lost. By the end of 1942 the Lancaster force was using its payload/range capability for attacks on targets in

Below: The seven-man crew of a Lancaster, seen here under the nose of a Mk I aeroplane, comprised the pilot, navigator, flight engineer, bomb-aimer, radio operator/gunner and two gunners.

northern Italy, where incendiary bomblets as well as 1814 and 3629kg (4000 and 8000lb) 'blockbuster' and 'cookie' bombs were carried over the Alps to be dropped on Genoa and Turin. Throughout this period bombing accuracy was not good, especially at night, but the situation was improved by better training and the introduction of new navigation and bombing equipment. The most important was the H2S navigation and target-location radar with its antenna in a semi-opaque Perspex radome under the fuselage to the rear of the bomb bay. H2S was first operated by No 49 Squadron in August 1943 and was then added to the aircraft of many other squadrons – except those of No 3 Group, whose Lancaster bombers had bulged bomb bay doors that precluded the addition of the radome.

Dams raid

The most celebrated of all Lancaster operations was without doubt the attack on the series of dams in western Germany above the Ruhr industrial region by aircraft of No 617 Squadron.

Undertaken on 16–17 May 1943, this operation had been set in motion on 26 February of the same year, once preliminary trials using half-scale versions of the special weapon developed by Dr. Barnes Wallis of Vickers-Armstrongs had shown that the attack was technically feasible. The 'hit list' for the operation included the Muohne, Eder, Sorpe, Ennepe and Lister dams. The conversion of 23 aircraft (including three prototype machines) was authorized, and the final development and manufacture of the special weapons needed for the operation were taken in hand. The 'bouncing bomb' was in fact a mine that rotated backward to skip over the surface of the water until it impacted with the dam wall. It was cylindrical, with a length of 1.52m (5ft), a diameter of 1.27m (4ft 2in) and a weight of 4196kg (9250lb) including 2994kg (6600lb) of explosive. The weapon was designed by Wallis to skip over the anti-torpedo nets with which the Germans had protected the faces of the dams, to hit the face and then roll down to the pre-determined depth of 30ft (9.1m), at which point a

hydrostatic pistol would detonate the bomb.

Destruction of the dams would, it was believed, severely disrupt the generation of hydro-electric power for the Ruhr area and also cause severe flooding in the valleys below the dams, especially if the operation was undertaken in May, when the mass of water behind the dams would be at its maximum. Bomber Command did not want to have its main bomber force disrupted or reduced by the removal of a squadron for this special operation so on 21 March 1943 a new unit, No 617 Squadron, was created for this specific task, using experienced crews drawn piecemeal from the front-line squadrons.

The modification of the Lancaster for the attack on the Ruhr dams included removal of the weapons bay doors, as the weapon would not fit in the bomb bay otherwise. To reduce weight the dorsal turret was also removed. The bomb was carried with its

Below: **Debriefing of the returning crews from the 'Dam Buster' raids.**

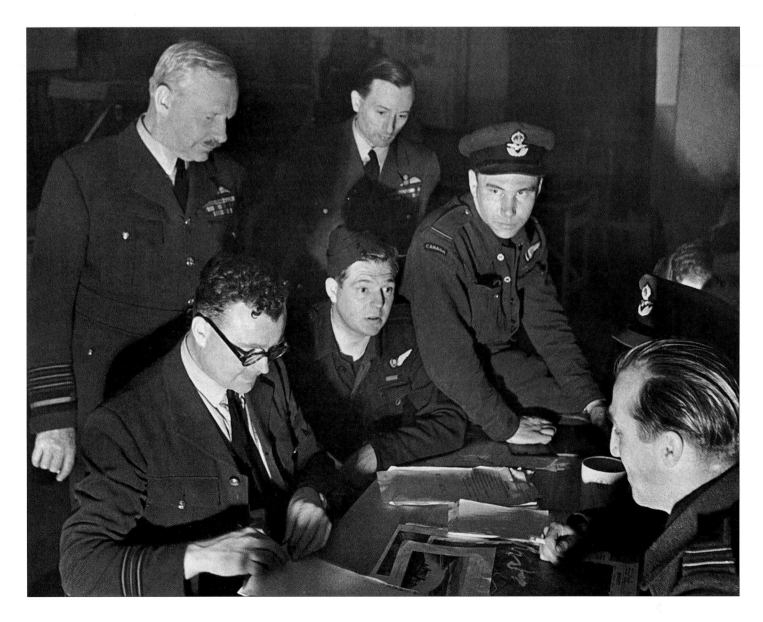

Right: The attack on the Ruhr
dams was led by Wing
Commander Guy Gibson, who
was awarded the Victoria Cross
for his gallantry on this
occasion.

axis of rotation across the aeroplane, suspended
between two V-shaped struts: a disc on each of these
struts matched a sunken circular track at each end of
the weapon. One of the discs was belt-driven to spin
the bomb to 500 rpm before release, and the
removal of the weapons bay doors and dorsal turret
meant that the bomber's standard hydraulic system
could be used to power the hydraulic pump and
spin the weapon.

The operation had to be flown at low level, with
bomb release at only 18.3m (60ft) above the water,
and other modifications to the bomber included a
trainable machine gun in the floor of the lower
fuselage to the rear of the bomb bay with a kneel-
ing pad for the gunner, fairings at the front and
rear of the bomb bay, and two specialized aiming
devices. One was a triangulation sight matched to
the distance between the towers at each end of the
dam to ensure weapons release came at 365–410m
(400–450 yards) from the dam. The other con-
sisted of two spotlights whose beams touched
together on the surface of the water when the

aeroplane was at exactly 18.3m (60ft).

All 23 aircraft converted to carry the 'bouncing
bomb' were Lancaster Mk III machines with Merlin
28 engines. The first of the three prototypes reached
the Royal Aircraft Establishment at Farnborough on
8 April 1943, the second was employed for weapon
release trials off Reculver on the coast of Kent, and
the third was despatched to the Aircraft &
Armament Experimental Establishment for handling trials. The first of the 20 'production' aircraft
was delivered to No 617 Squadron at RAF Scampton
on 18 April, and there followed a month of arduous
low-flying training by day and night.

One of the aircraft having been damaged on 10
May, there were 19 aircraft available for the operation on 15–16 May. The aircraft flew in three waves:
the first, under the command of Wing Commander
Guy Gibson, the squadron's commander, had nine
aircraft and the other two each comprised five aircraft. The first wave was to attack the two most
important targets, the Möhne dam and then the
Eder dam. The second wave was tasked with the

Left: The special 'bouncing bomb' designed for the raid on the Ruhr dams was 1.52m (5ft) in length and 1.27m (4ft 2in) in diameter, and was spun by a belt drive from a hydraulic motor to 500 rpm.

Below: The Lancaster Mk II differed from the Lancaster Mk I baseline model only in having a powerplant of four Bristol Hercules air-cooled radial engines rather than four Merlin liquid-cooled V-12 engines. This was an aeroplane of No 426 Squadron, and was lost during a raid on Stuttgart during 7 October 1943.

Below: The 'Tallboy' deep-penetration bomb, seen here on its special transporter, was more formally designated as 'Bomb, HE, Aircraft DP, 12,000lb' in September 1944 but soon changed to 'Bomb, HE, Aircraft, MC, 12,000lb'.

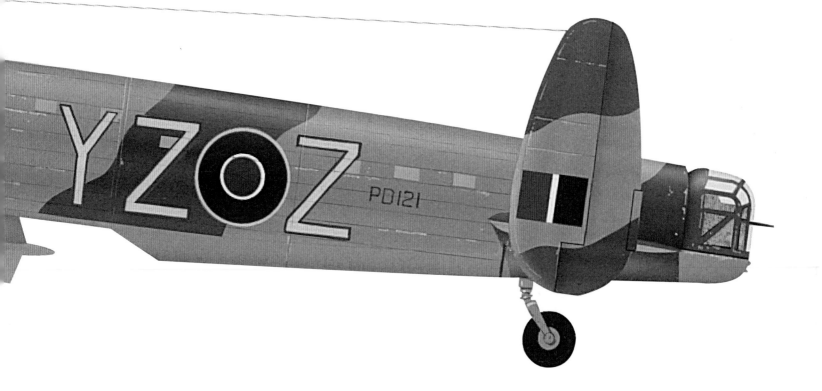

attack on the Sorpe dam. The third wave (the air-borne reserve) was also given the Sorpe as its target, with the Ennepe and Lister dams as secondary objectives.

In the event, only the aircraft of the first wave were fully successful. One of the aircraft was lost on the outward flight, and of the surviving eight machines five dropped their 'bouncing bombs' on the Möhne dam, breaching it, while the other three achieved the same result with the Eder dam. Two and one weapons were dropped on the Sorpe and Ennepe dams respectively, but caused no catastrophic breaches in them. Eight of the 19 aircraft were lost.

Tallboy

Back in the world of conventional bombing, the bulging of the bomb bay doors to carry the 3629kg (8000lb) 'blockbuster' or 'cookie' bomb was found to make these Lancaster bombers capable of carry-ing the 5443kg (12,000lb) weapon of the same high-capacity type. These bombs were made in

modules – three rather than two modules made the weapon longer but not broader. The bomb bay was also long enough to accommodate the 5443kg (12,000lb) 'Tallboy'. This streamlined deep-penetra-tion bomb, also designed by Wallis, was also carried by aircraft of No 617 Squadron, like the 'bouncing bomb'. 617 had relinquished its surviving 'dam buster' aircraft immediately after the attack of 15–16 May, but the squadron remained in existence and continued to extend its reputation and repertoire, particularly in specialized low-level operations.

One of No 617's first attacks with the 'Tallboy' bomb, which proved to be very effective, was on the Saumur railway tunnel. On the night of 8–9 June 1944, when the tunnel was collapsed, the Germans were moving reinforcements through it toward Normandy. On 11 September of the same year, a force of 38 Lancaster Mk I and Mk III bombers from Nos 617 and 9 Squadrons with their bomb bays modified for carriage of the 'Tallboy' bomb deployed to Yagodnik near Arkhangel'sk in the

Above: **No 617 Squadron started to receive the first of its 33 Lancaster B.Mk I (Special) aircraft in the spring of 1944. The aircraft were initially fitted with bulged weapons bay doors for the carriage and delivery of 'Tallboy' bombs, but the doors were removed from March 1945 so that the aircraft could carry and deliver the considerably larger 'Grand Slam' weapon.**

northern part of the USSR. This was to be the launching point for an attack on Germany's only modern battleship, the *Tirpitz*, then lying in the Altenfjord in northern Norway. The attack took place on 15 September, when a force of 27 Lancaster aircraft (21 of them each carrying one 'Tallboy' bomb and the other six each carrying one anti-ship bomb) scored hits on the great ship but failed to sink her.

In October 1944 the German navy moved the *Tirpitz* to a point near Tromsö, and this brought the ship within range of Lancaster aircraft operating from the northern part of the UK. The Lancaster aircraft of Nos 617 and 9 Squadrons therefore moved to RAF Lossiemouth, and on 29 October made their second effort to sink the battleship. All the 37 aircraft (18 each from Nos 9 and 617 Squadrons as well as one camera aeroplane provided by No 463 Squadron) were of the Lancaster Mk I type with Merlin 24 engines, no dorsal turrets, and additional fuel tanks in the fuselage raising total capacity to 10937.7 litres (2889.4 US gal; 2406 Imp gal). The aircraft dropped 32 'Tallboy' bombs but

made no hits. A third, successful attack followed on 12 November, when 38 Lancaster Mk I aircraft from the same squadrons took off again from Lossiemouth: 28 of the aircraft dropped their 'Tallboy' bombs over the German battleship, and the two that hit their target capsized it.

Grand Slam

The highly trained and experienced crews of Nos 9 and 617 Squadrons proved effective at the precisely accurate delivery required to give the 'Tallboy' bomb its greatest destructive effect, and it was crews of these two squadrons who delivered the majority of the 854 'Tallboy' bombs used operationally. When the conceptually similar but larger 'Grand Slam' weapon, weighing 9979kg (22,000lb) became available, it was only sensible to allocate one of the two specialist squadrons to the task of using the new bomb.

Work on the conversion of a first bomber to the required Lancaster Mk I (Special) standard started during October 1944 for flight trials from February of the following year. There followed another 32 production-standard conversions for which a maximum take-off weight of 32,660kg (72,000lb) was fixed. All the aircraft had Merlin 24 engines. They had the nose and dorsal turrets removed and the resulting openings faired over, and the bomb bays adapted for the huge bomb by the removal of the doors and the addition of front and rear fairings.

A Lancaster Mk I (Special) made the first release of a live 'Grand Slam' over a British test range on 13 March, and No 617 Squadron flew the first operation with this weapon on the following day. 15 bombers, 14 of them carrying 'Tallboy' weapons and one a 'Grand Slam', attacked and brought down the Bielefeld Viaduct. Aircraft of the same squadron dropped all the other 40 'Grand Slam' bombs used operationally in World War II, and the only other unit to operate the Lancaster Mk I (Special) was No 15 Squadron, which converted onto this model only after the end of the war.

Pathfinders

Most Lancaster squadrons were part of Bomber Command's Main Force but there were a small number of squadrons that operated in the important pathfinder role. The Pathfinder Force was established in August 1942 as No 8 (PFF) Group, and at first the group's strength of five squadrons included only one equipped with the Lancaster. This was No 83 Squadron, which had been transferred from No 5 Group. A second Lancaster unit was No 97 Squadron, which joined No 8 Group in the course of April 1943. Before the end of World War II

Nos 7, 35, 156, 405, 582 and 635 Squadrons had also come onto the strength of No 8 Group with aircraft of the Lancaster Mks I and III models. The aircraft retained the Lancaster's standard bomb bay layout, which was more than adequate for the carriage of the pyrotechnic bombs used as target indicators. But their navigation and bomb-aiming equipment was steadily upgraded to ensure that the master bombers provided by No 8 Group's bombers effectively found and marked the right targets for the bombers of the Main Force squadrons.

Far East

Although no units equipped with the Lancaster bomber became operational in either the Middle East or the Far East before the end of World War II, the Air Ministry started planning as early as 1943 for the deployment of the Lancaster to the Far East. In order to generate the data required to prepare a properly planned programme for tropicalization of the Lancaster, two Lancaster Mk I aircraft were allocated to No 1577 (Special Duties) Flight at Mauripur for one year from October 1943. In their time with this flight, the two aircraft undertook trials in the towing of Horsa and Hamilcar assault gliders within the context of a wide-ranging investigation into the feasibility of gliderborne operations in the Burma theatre.

A scheme to tropicalize the Lancaster was completed by the end of 1944, leading to the creation of new-build or converted Lancaster B.Mk I (FE) and B.Mk VII (FE) aircraft. It was intended that these

Below: During 1944 and 1945 RAF Bomber Command tore the heart out of Germany's capacity to wage and sustain a protracted war, especially after the decline of the German fighter arm allowed the bomber to operate by day as well as night, in the process adding pinpoint attack to their urban destruction roles.

aircraft should operate (together with the new Lincoln which was expected in the near future) as part of Tiger Force, the very long-range British bomber force tasked to operate against Japan. As the war against Japan ended in August 1945, Nos 83, 97, 106 and 207 Squadrons of the RAF, as well as No 467 Squadron of the Royal Australian Air Force and No

75 Squadron of the Royal New Zealand Air Force had been selected for service in the Pacific theatre with the FE Lancasters.

Berchtesgaden

The Lancaster's final bombing raids of the war took place on 25–26 April 1945. In the day, Nos 1, 5 and 8

Right: **A spectacular image of a pair of general-purpose bombs starting their journey from the weapons bay to the target, in this instance a base for Germany's feared and very capable U-boat arm.**

Groups put up a force of 375 aircraft comprising 16 de Havilland Mosquito twin-engined aircraft and 359 Lancaster bombers (including 16 of No 617 Squadron's aircraft carrying 'Tallboy' bombs) to attack Adolf Hitler's retreat at Berchtesgaden in southern Germany. The British aircraft were escorted by North American P-51 Mustang fighters of the US 8th Army Air Force and caused considerable damage for the loss of two Lancasters. On the night of the same day, No 5 Group sent 107 Lancaster bombers and 12 Mosquito aircraft to attack the U-boat oil storage tanks in Oslofjord. The raid was completed with great accuracy, resulting in significant damage to the tanks. The raid also resulted in the last of more than 3300 Lancaster losses in World War II: a bomber of No 463 Squadron was forced to make an emergency landing in neutral Sweden, and the crew was interned for the last few days of the war.

As well as their bombing raids, the Lancaster aircraft also undertook humanitarian operations in April 1945, which continued into the last month of the war. Each aircraft carried five panniers of food in its bomb bay to be dropped on Dutch towns, which were suffering a severe food shortage. More than 6000 tons of food were dropped in 3156 sorties. The Lancaster's final role in the last days of the war and first days of European peace was repatriation: in Operation 'Exodus' between 4 and 28 May, Lancaster aircraft carrying an average of 25 men in the fuselage brought back to the UK about 75,000 prisoners-of-war released from German camps.

Sea rescue

Right through World War II almost all Lancasters had been operated by Bomber Command. But after the end of the war reduced demand for the Lancaster coincided with imminent arrival of more

Above: **With their parachute packs lying on the tarmac in the foreground, members of a Lancaster crew wait for their aircraft to be prepared for take-off.**

Above: NX612 was a Lancaster B.Mk VII completed to FE (Far Eastern) standard, and was allocated to Nos 38, 32 and 20 Maintenance Units respectively. It ended its career in the French naval air service.

Below: This Lancaster B.Mk 3 was adapted for the maritime reconnaissance and air/sea rescue roles as a Lancaster ASR.Mk 3. This aeroplane was the last Lancaster in regular service with the Royal Air Force.

modern aircraft and the Air Ministry were persuaded to authorize the development of the Lancaster for the air/sea rescue role, principally for operations in the Pacific. The air-dropped lifeboat had been developed for use first by the Lockheed Hudson and then by the Vickers Warwick ASR.Mk III. Now, in its Mk II form, this lifeboat was adapted for the Lancaster, which could be fitted with a single-point attachment for the lifeboat under the bomb bay.

Some Lancaster Mk III aircraft were adapted to the new role at the Eastleigh facility of Cunliffe Owen Aircraft, receiving the designation Lancaster ASR.Mk 3. The first operational unit with this model was No 279 Squadron, based at RAF St Eval.

The Lancaster ASR.Mk 3 was also used from home bases by Nos 120, 203, 310 and 224 Squadrons in Coastal Command, and by Nos 37, 38 and 621 Squadrons in the Middle East. Another role undertaken by Lancaster aircraft of Coastal Command was general reconnaissance, leading to the further conversion of about 100 Lancaster ASR.Mk 3 aircraft as Lancaster GR.Mk 3 machines. These aircraft were operated by Nos 120, 203 and 210 Squadrons from home bases and Nos 37 and 38 Squadrons from Maltese bases. The Lancaster GR.Mk 3 retained the Lancaster ASR.Mk 3's facility for carriage of the Mk II or Mk IIa lifeboat, but added to this ASV.Mk III surface-search radar (with a radome based on that of the H2S radar equipment) and had

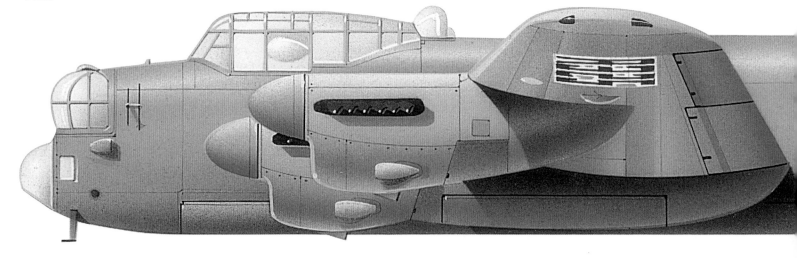

Left: Air/sea rescue Lancaster
ASR/GR.Mk 3 undergoes
checks at an unidentified
airfield in the Far East,
watched by a huge crowd of
spectators.

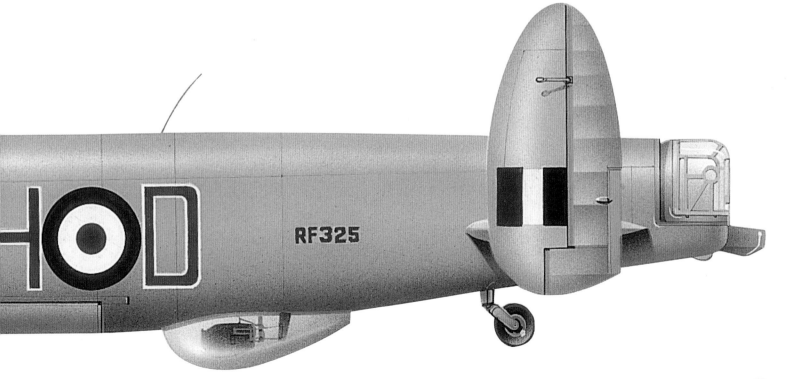

RF325

no dorsal turret. By the time one of these aircraft made the last flight by an operational Lancaster in British service on 15 October 1956, the Lancaster GR.Mk 3 had been redesignated as the Lancaster MR.Mk 3.

Another post-war variant, flown only by No 82 Squadron, was the Lancaster PR.Mk 1. This had its nose and tail turrets removed, and its bomb bay converted to carry cameras. Lancaster PR.Mk 1 aircraft were used mainly for aerial survey, and in this capacity completed a large-scale survey of East, Central and West Africa between 1946 and the end of 1952.

The Lancaster remained in service with the RAF as a bomber until March 1950, when No 49 Squadron converted to the Lincoln as the last of post-war Lancaster bomber units that had also included Nos 101, 115, 138, 148, 149, 207 and 214 Squadrons at home with Lancaster B.Mk 1 and B.Mk 3 aircraft, Nos 9 and 617 Squadron in India with Lancaster B.Mk 7 (FE) aircraft, and Nos 37, 40 and 104 Squadrons in the Middle East with

Lancasters of the same variant.

Using the Canadian-built Lancaster Mk X (or Mk 10 as it now was), the Royal Canadian Air Force produced a number of variants to meet their particular requirements. A total of 230 Lancaster aircraft featured on the RCAF's strength between the end of World War II and the retirement of the last aeroplane in April 1964. The main Canadian models were 13 and 72 examples respectively of the bomber/reconnaissance Lancaster Mk 10-BR and maritime reconnaissance Lancaster Mk 10-MR. Many Lancaster Mk 10-MR aircraft were later redesignated as maritime patrol Lancaster Mk 10-MP aircraft. Other Canadian models were eight air/sea rescue Lancaster Mk 10-SR aircraft, 11 photoreconnaissance Lancaster Mk 10-P aircraft, three navigation training Lancaster Mk 10-N aircraft and two drone-carrying Lancaster Mk 10-DC aircraft.

Almost all the Lancaster bombers that lasted to the end of World War II in the UK were then scrapped. Small numbers of aircraft did survive, however, and this was fortunate, as there emerged a

small export market for the aircraft in the late 1940s. In 1948 Avro bought 24 Lancaster B.Mk 1 aircraft from the RAF and refurbished them for sale to the Argentine and Egyptian air forces, which received 15 and nine aircraft respectively. In 1952 the company converted 31 Lancaster B.Mk 1 and 22 Lancaster B.Mk 7 aircraft to maritime reconnaissance standard for delivery to the French naval air arm, which operated the aircraft up to 1961 from bases in southern France and northern Africa, and also from Nouméa in the South Pacific until 1964.

But it is as a bomber that the Lancaster makes its claim to immortality, and of the two airworthy Lancaster aircraft that survive into the 21st century, pride of place must go to a former Lancaster PR.Mk 1 restored to the standard of the Lancaster B.Mk I, now maintained by the RAF's Battle of Britain Memorial Flight.

Above: **A Lancaster PR.Mk I surveying East Africa in 1948.**

Below: **French naval air service Lancasters had their dorsal turret removed, additional fuel tanks added, and provision made for ASV (Air-to-Surface) search radar and an airborne lifeboat.**

Left: Maintained in immaculate condition and bearing the letter code of No 103 Squadron, the 'City of Lincoln' is the pride and joy of the Royal Air Force's Battle of Britain Memorial Flight.

CHAPTER FIVE

Transport and Bomber Developments

From the beginning of its career, the Lancaster bomber revealed that it could carry a significant warload over long ranges at comparatively high speed. This suggested to the Avro design team that a pure transport derivative could be evolved without undue difficulty.

Roy Chadwick's team completed the drawings of the new type in February 1942, and the Type 685 first prototype made its maiden flight in July 1942 as the marriage of the flying surfaces, landing gear and powerplant of the Lancaster Mk I bomber to a new semi-monocoque tapered fuselage. The new fuselage provided about double the cubic capacity of the Lancaster, and the payload was carried in a small forward and larger rear cabin separated by the port-side door with the lavatory opposite it; behind the main cabin was provision for a galley and a baggage compartment.

York

Just before the first Type 685 flew, Avro received a contract for four prototypes and a small number of production aircraft to be finished in passenger transport configuration. The first prototype was completed as a freight transport, the second as a passenger transport with round cabin windows, the third as passenger transport with square cabin windows, and the fourth as a paratroop transport with dropping doors in the floor of the fuselage. The turbulence of the airflow along the fuselage was found to make the type unsuitable for the paratrooping role, however, and no further aircraft of this type were built.

The first machine was used for trials and was later converted into the York C.Mk 2 prototype with four 1230kW (1650hp) Bristol Hercules VI radial

engines. Avro retained the second for development work, and the third was refurbished as a VIP transport with a conference room. This last machine was delivered in March 1943 to No 24 Squadron as the first York C.Mk 1, and became the personal transport of Prime Minister Winston Churchill.

From the third prototype onward, the tail unit inherited from the Lancaster was supplemented by a fixed fin above the fuselage to improve directional stability, which had been adversely affected by the new fuselage's greater keel area forward of the centre of gravity. The production priority enjoyed by the Lancaster bomber meant deliveries of the York

Opposite: A special flight of steps is necessary to reach the nose mail compartment of this BOAC Lancastrian.

Below: The York C.Mk 1 was a comparatively straightforward transport development of the Lancaster, with the addition of a centreline fin and the introduction of a new square-section fuselage that carried the wing in the shoulder-set position.

C.Mk 1 were initially slow, and the type began to enter full squadron service only in May 1944. The first unit to be equipped solely with the York C.Mk 1 was No 511 Squadron which received the type in 1945, but by the time construction ended in April 1948 after the delivery of 208 military aircraft, Royal Air Force Transport Command had a total of ten squadrons flying Yorks. Seven of these squadrons played an invaluable part in the Berlin Airlift that started in July 1948 as the western Allies kept West Berlin supplied with essential fuel, food and other supplies in the face of a Soviet blockade of the city.

The aircraft operated by the RAF were delivered in three configurations as passenger transport, freight transport and passenger/freight transport aircraft. The York C.Mk 1 was gradually replaced by the Handley Page H.P.67 Hastings from late 1948, but the last aircraft were not retired until 1957. Surplus aircraft were generally snapped up by airlines and charter operators to supplement the 49 similar aircraft built for the civil market.

Lancastrian

While the Type 691 Lancastrian is remembered mainly for its use after World War II at a time when the UK was very short of transport aircraft, it is often overlooked that the machine originated in Canada when, in 1942, a British-built Lancaster B.Mk III was stripped of its turrets and camouflage by Victory Aircraft of Toronto, who fitted it with pointed nose and tail fairings, plus three extra windows: such a type, offering long range but only modest capacity, was needed for the return westward to Canada of ferry crews who had just completed an eastward crossing of the Atlantic to deliver aircraft from Canada to the USA. Trans Canada Airlines evaluated the machine for freight services between Moncton and Goose Bay, a distance of some 853km (460nm; 530 miles), and found the performance and load-carrying capabilities satisfactory. Such was the requirement for high-speed transports that this modified Lancaster was returned to Avro in the UK for more permanent conversion which involved, among other things, the fitting of ten passenger seats and the installation of extra fuel tanks to increase the range to 6437km (3474nm; 4000 miles). In its new form the aircraft inaugurated the Canadian government's transat-

Right: The inside of the York C.Mk 1's fuselage gave the passenger no clue that the aeroplane was derived from the Lancaster bomber.

lantic air service (operated by TCA) on 22 July 1943 with four tons of forces' mail.

The British certificate of airworthiness was granted on 1 September 1943, and TCA initiated conversion of two (later seven) Canadian-built Lancaster B.Mk X aircraft. One was lost over the Atlantic in December 1944, and the original conversion was destroyed by fire while engaged in engine trials in June 1945; but the remaining Lancaster aircraft continued to operate the Atlantic route as a scheduled passenger service. The aircraft proved uneconomical in this task, and were replaced in 1947 by Lockheed Constellations after making 1900 crossings of the Atlantic.

Problems with the Avro Tudor, ordered by the British Overseas Airways Corporation for its Australian service, encouraged Avro to undertake conversion of 20 Lancaster aircraft from the end of its production line. This involved a more detailed conversion than the Canadian aircraft, and the designation Type 691 Lancastrian was adopted. With 2273 litre (600.5 US gal; 500 Imp gal) fuel tanks in the bomb bay, the Lancastrian had a range of well over

AVRO YORK C.MK 1

Type: long-range transport aeroplane

Crew: flight crew of five on an enclosed flight deck, and up to 24 passengers or 4536kg (10,000lb) of freight carried in two payload compartments

Armament: none

Powerplant: four Rolls-Royce Merlin T.24 liquid-cooled Vee piston engines each rated at 1208kW (1620hp) for take-off

Fuel: internal 11265 litres (2975.9 US gal; 2478 Imp gal); external none

Wing: span 31.09m (102ft); aspect ratio 8.02; area 120.49 sq m (1297 sq ft)

Fuselage and tail: length 23.93m (78ft 6in); height 5.44m (17ft 10in); tailplane span 10.06m (33ft)

Weights: empty 19,069kg (42,040lb); maximum take-off 31,115kg (68,597lb)

Performance: maximum speed 'clean' 480km/h (259kt; 298 mph) at 6400m (21,000ft); cruising speed 338km/h (182kt; 210 mph) at optimum altitude; initial climb rate 457m (1500ft) per minute; service ceiling 7010m (23,000ft); typical range 4345km (2345nm; 2700 miles)

Below: The York C.Mk 1 offered adequate performance in terms of speed and range, but was nowhere near rival American transports in terms of capacity and operating economy.

Above: The Lancastrian was a simpler evolution of the Lancaster into a transport than that represented by the York, but was both cheap and quick to develop. The aircraft played an important part in the Berlin Airlift that began in 1948 as the Soviets tried to starve out the sectors of the city occupied by the Western powers.

AVRO LANCASTRIAN C.MK 2

Type: long-range transport aeroplane

Crew: flight crew of three or four on the enclosed flight deck, and up to nine passengers in an enclosed cabin

Armament: none

Powerplant: four Rolls-Royce Merlin T.24/2 liquid-cooled Vee piston engines each rated at 1219kW (1635hp) for take-off

Fuel: internal not available; external none

Wing: span 31.09m (102ft); area 120.49 sq m (1297.00 sq ft) Fuselage and tail: length 23.42m (76ft 10in); height 5.94m (19ft 6in)

Weights: empty 13,801kg (30,426lb); maximum take-off 29,484kg (65,000lb)

Performance: maximum speed 'clean' 499km/h (269kt; 310 mph) at 3660m (12,000ft); cruising speed 370km/h (200kt; 230 mph) at 5335m (17,500ft); initial climb rate 229m (750ft) per minute; service ceiling 9145m (30,000ft); range 6679km (3604nm; 4150 miles)

6437km (3474nm; 4000 miles), and the first aeroplane to be handed over early in 1945 established a record between the UK and New Zealand of three and a half days. Operations were undertaken jointly on the Commonwealth routes with Qantas, although the aircraft were flown initially in RAF markings with the designation Lancastrian C.Mk 1. One Lancastrian was lost over the sea in March 1946, but although the type was uneconomical to operate, prestige demanded the retention of this fast route.

Following proving trials with a BOAC Lancastrian 1 on the South Atlantic route, an order was placed for six Lancastrian 3 aircraft for the new British South American Airways, to begin operations in 1946. These aircraft had better accommodation, for 13 passengers. With the basic type proved on civil routes, Avro received an order for the Lancastrian C.Mk 2 for the Royal Air Force. Basically similar to the civil Lancastrian 1 but with nine seats, the Lancastrian C.Mk 2 entered service in October 1945. 33 of these aircraft were supplied, fol-

Above: VM734 was one of a batch of 18 Lancastrian C.Mk II transport aircraft ordered from A.V. Roe Ltd during February 1945 and delivered between October 1945 and February 1946 with Merlin 24 engines.

Left: G-AHJV was one of two Lancaster B.Mk 3s converted to form the tanker element of an inflight-refuelling system, another two being adapted with the receiver element. The aircraft were used by British South American Airways to ensure safe long-range passage over the Atlantic Ocean.

lowed by 18 of the 10–13-seat Lancastrian C.Mk 4 (equivalent to the civil Lancastrian 3). The aircraft were used by No 24 Squadron and the Empire Air Navigation School.

In all respects, the BSAA operation to South America proved unfortunate. Of the six Lancastrian transports bought, four crashed between August 1946 and November 1947, the other two were sold, and two of the Tudors that replaced the Lancastrian aircraft disappeared en route. BSAA was later absorbed by BOAC, and a further 12 Lancastrian 3 aircraft were delivered to other customers including Alitalia, Qantas, Silver City Airways and Skyways. The independent operators made considerable use of Lancastrian transports, particularly during the Berlin Airlift, when they were used as tankers for petrol and Diesel oil, with a capacity of 11,365 litres (3002.3 US gal; 2500 Imp gal).

Most of the RAF's surviving Lancastrian aircraft later found their way onto the civil market, but a number served as engine test-beds. The first of these, converted by Rolls-Royce in 1946, was used with two Rolls-Royce Nene turbojet engines in the outboard engine positions, and it became the first commercial type in the world to fly solely on jet power when the piston engines in the two inboard positions were stopped. Flying on just the Nene engines, the Lancastrian covered the route from London to Paris in 50 minutes in November 1946. Another Nene test-bed followed, then five more machines to test the de Havilland Ghost, Rolls-Royce Avon and Armstrong Siddeley Sapphire engines. Two more were converted for piston engine test work with Rolls-Royce Griffon 57 units inboard and Merlin T.24/4 units outboard.

A total of 82 Lancastrian aircraft were built in the UK, plus nine in Canada.

Lincoln

In 1943 Bomber Command was still heavily involved in the nocturnal strategic bombing cam-

Below: **Both the Lancaster and the Lincoln were used as test-beds for advanced turbine engines, including those of the Armstrong Siddeley company. The Mamba turboprop and the Adder and Viper turbojets were trialled in a Lancaster, while the Python turboprop was tested in a Lincoln.**

paign against Germany with the Lancaster and Halifax as its primary warplanes. But the Air Ministry were already considering the part the RAF would play in the strategic air campaign against Japan after Germany had been defeated. Although well satisfied with the performance and overall capabilities of the Lancaster, the RAF's planners appreciated that it lacked the range and defensive armament for effective use against Japan. In 1943, therefore, the RAF issued its specification B14/43 for a bomber to succeed the Lancaster. It stipulated four Rolls-Royce Merlin engines with two-speed superchargers to give a cruising altitude of 10,670m (35,000ft) and improved range without any degradation of bomb load.

The Avro design team under Roy Chadwick had already begun to consider a new bomber on the aerodynamic and structural basis of the Lancaster, and the design for the improved bomber began to take shape with the company designation Type 694. This was based on a longer-span wing of higher aspect ratio, a lengthened fuselage with a new nose, a modified bomb bay, and beefed-up landing gear.

The Air Ministry was impressed with the new design and planned to order two variants – the Lancaster B.Mk IV with four 1253kW (1680hp) Merlin 85 engines, and the Lancaster B.Mk V with four 1305kW (1750hp) Merlin 68 engines. A number of Lancaster components and assemblies were used in the new bomber, but the RAF eventually recognized the nature of the wholesale changes and decided that the Merlin 85-engined model should be renamed the Lincoln B.Mk 1.

Cutbacks

The first of three prototypes made its maiden flight on 9 June 1944, and flight trials showed excellent performance and good handling. Plans were laid for the production of 2254 aircraft in five factories

Below: **VH742 was one of two Lancastrian Mk IV aircraft built specifically as test-beds for the Rolls-Royce RB41 Nene turbojet, of which two examples were installed in the outer nacelles. Here the aeroplane is flying on turbojet power alone, the two Merlin engines being stopped and their propellers feathered.**

Right: RE228 was a Lincoln B.Mk 1 used by Rolls-Royce for engine tests with the standard Merlin 85 engines replaced by Merlin T.85 units.

Below: Seen at the Anti-Submarine Warfare Development Unit are P9, a Lancaster B.Mk 1 (PB809) struck off charge in March 1948, and HW-A, a Lincoln of No 100 Squadron.

operated by three companies, and the first Lincoln B.Mk 1 came off the production line in February 1945. The Lincoln entered service in September 1945, the month in which the Japanese signed their surrender, and with the loss of the new bomber's operating theatre the RAF curtailed production of this initial model to just 72 aircraft. These remained in service only to 1946 before being relegated to second-line duties and then retirement in February 1949.

Apart from its powerplant, the only way in which the Lincoln B.Mk 1 differed from the definitive Lincoln B.Mk 2 was in its defensive armament, which comprised six 12.7mm (0.5in) Browning machine guns in three power-operated two-gun turrets: a Boulton Paul Type F nose turret, a Martin (later Bristol Type 17) dorsal turret, and a Frazer-Nash F.N.82 tail turret (preceded in some aircraft by the F.N.121 turret with four 7.7mm (0.303in) Browning machine guns). Provision was also made for an F.N.88 ventral turret, but this was never installed.

The Lincoln B.Mk 2 was the definitive model, with American-built engines and the defensive armament significantly enhanced by the installation of two 20mm (0.8in) cannon in the dorsal turret for greater effective range and hitting power against attacking fighters. Production for the RAF totalled 477 aircraft, but 12 of these were diverted in 1947 to Argentina, whose air force also received 18 newly-built aircraft. All the aircraft had been delivered by April 1951, and by June 1948 the earlier aircraft had been tropicalized in recognition of the fact that their range suited them to overseas deployments in theatres like the Far East.

By 1947 the Lincoln B.Mk 2 aircraft had been equipped to two standards. Those designated Lincoln B.Mk 2/IIIG had H2S Mk IIIG radar and well as 'Gee Mk II' and 'Rebecca Mk II' navigation systems, while those designated Lincoln B.Mk 2/IVA had H2S Mk IVA radar as well as 'Gee-H Mk II' and 'Rebecca Mk II' or 'Rebecca Mk IV' navigation systems. The last aircraft had been retired from first-line service by 1955, when the Vickers Valiant turbojet-powered bomber became the RAF's premier bomber.

Variants

There were also several unbuilt or limited-service Lincoln variants. The Lincoln B.Mk 3 was projected in 1945 with a saddle tank between the cockpit and the dorsal turret for very long range, but the Mk 3

Above: RF385 was a Lincoln B.Mk 1 in service with No 57 Squadron. The family resemblance to the Lancaster is quite unmistakable.

designation was then switched to a general reconnaissance type that eventually matured as the Avro (later Hawker Siddeley) Shackleton. The designation Lincoln B.Mk 4 was allocated to Lincoln B.Mk 2 bombers temporarily fitted with Merlin 85 engines, but it seems the designation was never actually used. The designation Lincoln U.Mk 5 was allocated to two drone conversions of which only one was flown. The Lincoln B.Mk XV was the Canadian-built model by Victory Aircraft, and was basically the Lincoln B.Mk 2 with Merlin 68A engines and a Martin model 23A dorsal turret. Only one of these machines was completed. The rest of the planned production was cancelled after Japan's surrender in 1945.

The Lincoln B.Mk 30 was the version of the Lincoln built in Australia by the Beaufort Division of the Australian Department of Aircraft Production. The first five aircraft were assembled from British-supplied components, the initial machine flying in March 1946. Australia had

planned to build 85 aircraft, but this total was later trimmed to 73 including 54 Lincoln B.Mk 30s. The first 24 aircraft were fitted with imported Merlin 85B engines, but the last 30 were completed with Australian-built Government Aircraft Factory (Rolls-Royce) Merlin 102 engines and the revised designation Lincoln B.Mk 30A. Australian engines were later retrofitted in the earlier aircraft to produce the Lincoln B.Mk 30A(B) variant. Nine of the aircraft were lost in crashes, and the surviving machines were all retired in 1961.

The Lincoln MR.Mk 31 designation was applied to the last 19 of the 73 Australian aircraft, which were completed to a maritime reconnaissance standard with the nose lengthened by 1.98m (6ft 6in) to provide accommodation for radar and its two operators. The aircraft were completed with full defensive armament, but in service the three turrets were generally removed. Two of the aircraft were lost in crashes, and the survivors were all retired in 1961.

Shackleton

Experience in World War II proved beyond doubt that the maritime reconnaissance warplane that offered the best possible combination of reliability, payload and performance was the four-engined landplane. After the war, the RAF's prime aircraft in this exacting role was the Lancaster GR.Mk 3 (later Lancaster MR.Mk 3), a development of the classic wartime night bomber that was on the verge of obsolescence even as it entered service.

In 1946, therefore, specification R5/46 was issued for a successor, and Avro proposed a Type 696 Lincoln GR.Mk 3 derivative of its Type 694 Lincoln heavy bomber, itself derived from the Lancaster design. But as the Type 696 design evolved it began to differ from the Lincoln sufficiently to warrant a new name, and the name Shackleton was selected. The new aircraft retained the wing and retractable tailwheel landing gear of the Lincoln, married to four Rolls-Royce Griffon Vee engines each driving a six-blade contra-rotating propeller unit. This wing and powerplant were combined with a new fuselage that was shorter but of greater cross-section than

that of the Lincoln, and carried the revised tail unit (with rounder vertical surfaces) in the high rather than mid/low position. Three prototypes were ordered, and the first of these flew on 9 March 1949, with the impressive armament of six 20mm (0.8in) cannon; one in each of two nose positions, and two each in dorsal and tail turrets.

The type was revised for production as the Shackleton GR.Mk 1 (later Shackleton MR.Mk 1) with a crew of ten, an internal warload of bombs and/or depth charges, gun armament revised to four 20mm (0.8in) cannon (two in the nose and two in the dorsal turret) and two 12.7 mm (0.5 in) heavy machine guns in the tail, and four Griffon engines (two Griffon Mk 57As and two Griffon Mk 57s). The first such machine flew in October 1950, and the type entered service in February 1951. Production totalled 77 aircraft, the later machines being delivered to Shackleton MR.1A standard with four Griffon Mk 57A engines, empty weight of 24,721kg (54,500lb), and maximum take-off weight of 39,010kg (86,000lb).

First flown in June 1952 for service from later in

Left: The serial number identifies this aeroplane as a Lincoln B.Mk 2, the final production model of the Lincoln from the British parent company.

Above: This Lincoln B.Mk 2 was operated by No 100 Squadron, based at RAF Hemswell between November 1946 and March 1950. It was deployed to Malaya in May of the latter year as part of the British air effort against the communist insurgents of the Malayan Emergency, and in 1954 the squadron spent two months in Kenya bombing the base areas of the Mau Mau terrorist group.

the same year, the Shackleton MR.Mk 2 variant was developed to improve on the radar performance of the Shackleton MR.Mk 1. The fuselage was lengthened and the chin radome of the Shackleton MR.Mk 1 was replaced by a semi-retractable radome in the ventral position. Radar performance was improved to a significant degree, and the revision of the fuselage included a new forward section with two 20mm cannon in a more effective installation above the bombardier's oblique window. A longer tail ending in a glazed tail cone replaced the tail guns, and the landing gear was also improved with a retractable twin-wheel tail unit replacing the original fixed single-wheel unit.

The defensive armament of the Shackleton MR.Mk 2 was based on pairs of 20mm (0.8in) trainable cannon in the nose position and dorsal turret, while the offensive armament was up to 6350kg (14,000lb) of bombs or other weapons carried in a lower-fuselage bomb bay and generally comprising mines, depth charges, and 454 and 227kg (1000 and 500lb) bombs as well as sonobuoys. Production of 59 aircraft was completed in September 1954, and from 1962 a number of the aircraft were revised to Shackleton MR.Mk 2C standard with the nav/attack

system of the Shackleton MR.Mk 3.

Into the '90s

Created by the conversion of 12 surplus Shackleton MR.Mk 2 airframes between 1971 and 1974, the Shackleton AEW.Mk 2 was fitted with the APS-20 radar stripped from Fairey Gannet AEW.Mk 3 aircraft, and provided the RAF with its sole airborne early warning capability in the period up to the arrival of the Boeing Sentry AEW.Mk 1 in 1992, when this last descendant of the Manchester and Lancaster finally disappeared from operational service.

The Shackleton MR.Mk 3 was the last production variant, and resulted from the need for an improved model able to assume the deep-ocean patrol tasking of the Short Sunderland flying boats that the RAF was phasing out of service. First flown in September 1955, the Shackleton MR.Mk 3 was clearly derived from the MR.Mk 2 but introduced a number of important enhancements. These included tricycle landing gear with a twin-wheel nose unit complementing new twin-wheel main units, deletion of the dorsal turret, tip tanks that raised the variant's internal fuel capac-

AVRO LINCOLN B.MK 2

Type: long-range heavy bomber

Crew: pilot and co-pilot/flight engineer side by side on the enclosed flight deck, and navigator, radio operator, bomb-aimer/gunner and two gunners carried in the fuselage

Armament (defensive): two 20mm Hispano No 4 Mk 5 cannon with 722 rounds in the power-operated Bristol Type 17 Mk II dorsal turret, two 12.7mm (0.5in) Browning trainable machine guns with 460 rounds in the power-operated Boulton Paul Type F Mk 1 nose turret, and two 12.7mm (0.5in) Browning trainable rearward-firing machine guns with 3040 rounds in the power-operated Boulton Paul Type D Mk 1 tail turret

Armament (offensive): up to 6350kg (14,000lb) standard or 10,206kg (22,500lb) maximum of bombs or other weapons carried in a lower-fuselage bomb bay rated at 10,206kg (22,500lb) and generally comprising one 10,206kg (22,500lb) 'Grand Slam' free-fall bomb or 14 454kg (1000lb) free-fall bombs

Powerplant: four Packard (Rolls-Royce) Merlin 68A liquid-cooled Vee piston engines each rated at 1286kW (1725hp) for take-off, 1323.5kW (1775hp) at 1220m (4000ft) and 1234kW (1655hp) at 5030m (16,500ft)

Fuel: internal 12,956.1 litres (3422.7 US gal; 2850 Imp gal) plus provision for up to 3636.8 litres (960.75 US gal; 800 Imp gal) in two optional 1818.4 litre (480.4 US gal; 400 Imp gal) weapons bay tanks; external none

Wing span: 36.58m (120ft); aspect ratio 10.13; area 132.01 sq m (1421 sq ft)

Fuselage and tail: length 23.86m (78ft 3.5in); height 5.27m (17ft 3.5in) with the tail down and 6.25m (20ft 6in) with the tail up; tailplane span 10.29m (33ft 9in); wheel track 7.24m (23ft 9in)

Weights: empty 20,044kg (44,188lb); normal take-off 34,020kg (75,000lb); maximum take-off 37,195kg (82,000lb)

Performance: maximum speed 'clean' 491km/h (265kt; 305 mph) at 5790m (19,000ft) declining to 380 km/h (205kt; 236 mph) at sea level; cruising speed 418.5 km/h (226kt; 260 mph) at 6095m (20,000 ft); initial climb rate 250m (820ft) per minute; climb to 6095m (20,000ft) in 30 minutes 0 seconds; service ceiling 8535m (28,000ft); range 7161km (3865nm; 4450 miles) with a 1361kg (3000lb) bomb load, or 4503km (2430nm; 2798 miles) with a 6350kg (14,000lb) bomb load, or 2177km (1175nm; 1353 miles) with a 10,206kg (22,500lb) bomb load

ity for still further range and/or endurance, modified ailerons, a wing of revised planform with underwing hardpoints for the carriage of additional weapons (most notably unguided rockets), a new frameless canopy for the pilot and co-pilot, and a sound-proofed wardroom so that off-duty members of the crew (two pilots, two navigators, one flight engineer, and five system operators) could rest more effectively.

42 aircraft were produced, including eight supplied to South Africa, and the type entered service late in 1957. From 1966 the surviving aircraft were upgraded by structural strengthening, by adding fuel capacity, and by installing two Rolls-Royce Viper ASV.11 Mk 203 turbojet engines.

The Shackleton T.Mk 4 designation was applied to a small number of Shackleton MR.Mk 1 aircraft converted for service from 1957 in the navigator training role.

Below: **The first production variant of the Shackleton for maritime reconnaissance was the Shackleton MR.Mk 1. This is VP258, the fifth production aeroplane, seen during a pre-delivery test flight over the Irish Sea off the coast of Lancashire.**

AVRO (HAWKER SIDDELEY/BRITISH AEROSPACE) SHACKLETON AEW.MK 2

Type: airborne early warning aeroplane

Crew: flight crew of four on the enclosed flight deck, and a crew of six carried in the cabin

Armament: none

Powerplant: four Rolls-Royce Griffon Mk 57A liquid-cooled Vee piston engines each rated at 1831kW (2455hp) for take-off with water/methanol injection

Fuel: internal not available; external none

Wing: span 36.58m (120ft); aspect ratio 10.13; area 132.01 sq m (1421.00 sq ft)

Fuselage and tail: length 26.62m (87ft 7in); height 5.10m (16ft 9in); tailplane span 10.06m (33ft); wheel track 7.24m (23ft 9in)

Weights: empty 25,855kg (57,000lb); maximum take-off 44,453kg (98,000lb)

Performance: maximum speed 'clean' 439 km/h (237kt; 273 mph) at optimum altitude; cruising speed not available; initial climb rate 259m (850ft) per minute; service ceiling 7010m (23,000ft); ferry range 6440km (3475nm; 4001 miles); range 4911km (2650nm; 3051 miles); endurance 14 hours 0 minutes

Left: The final descendant of the Lancaster in service anywhere in the world was the Shackleton AEW.Mk 2, an airborne early warning conversion from Shackleton MR.Mk 3 standard with the APS-20 radar using an antenna in the 'guppy' radome under the forward fuselage.

Below: The Shackleton AEW.Mk 2 was produced by conversion from Shackleton MR.Mk 2 standard, this being preferred to the more modern Shackleton MR.Mk 3 as it had tailwheel rather than tricycle landing gear, and consequently greater ground clearance for the APS-20 radar's radome.

Left: Though optimized for the maritime reconnaissance role, the Shackleton MR.Mk 2 could also be operated in the air/sea rescue role with the weapons bay adapted for the carriage and release of a parachute-dropped lifeboat stocked with food, water and radio equipment. The standard gun armament, introduced in the Mk 2 version, was a pair of 20mm cannon intended for the suppression of light anti-aircraft weapons on the decks of submarines and attacks on light warships.

Appendices

The Avro Lancaster in RAF Service

World War II
(first delivery/base/group/fuselage code)
by date of receipt of first aeroplane

No 44 (Rhodesian) Squadron
(December 1941/Waddington/No 5/KM)

No 97 Squadron
(January 1942/Coningsby/Nos 5 and 8/OF)

No 207 Squadron
(March 1942/Bottesford/No 5/EM)

No 83 Squadron
(April 1942/Coningsby/Nos 5 and 8/OL)

No 106 Squadron
(April 1942/Coningsby/No 5/ZN)

No 50 Squadron
(May 1942/Skellingthorpe/No 5/VN)

No 61 Squadron
(May 1942/Syerston/No 5/QR)

No 49 Squadron
(July 1942/Scampton/Nos 5, 3 and 1/EA)

No 9 Squadron
(August 1942/Waddington/No 5/WS)

No 57 Squadron
(September 1942/Scampton/No 5/DX)

No 460 (Australian) Squadron
(October 1942/Breighton/No 1/UV and AR)

No 101 Squadron
(October 1942/Holme-on-Spalding Moor/No 1/SR)

No 103 Squadron
(November 1942/Elsham Wolds/No 1/PM)

No 12 Squadron
(November 1942/Wickenby/No 1/PH)

No 467 (Australian) Squadron
(November 1942/Scampton/No 5/PO)

No 156 Squadron
(December 1942/Warboys/No 8/GT)

No 100 Squadron
(December 1942/Grimsby/No 1/HW)

No 115 Squadron
(March 1943/East Wretham/No 3/KO, AA and IL)

No 617 Squadron
(March 1943/Scampton/No 5/AJ, KC and YZ)

No 619 Squadron
(April 1943/Woodhall Spa/No 5/PG)

No 7 Squadron
(May 1943/Oakington/Nos 85 and 3/MG and XU)

No 426 (Canadian) Squadron
(June 1943/Linton-on-Ouse/No 6/KW)

No 405 (Canadian) Squadron
(August 1943/Gransden Lodge/Nos 8
and 6/LQ and AG)

No 408 (Canadian) Squadron
(August 1943/Linton-on-Ouse/No 6/EQ,
AK and MN)

No 166 Squadron
(September 1943/Kirmington/No 1/AS)

No 514 Squadron
(September 1943/Foulsham/No 3/JI and A2)

No 625 Squadron
(October 1943/Kelstern/No 1/CF)

No 550 Squadron
(October 1945/Grimsby/No 1/BQ)

No 432 (Canadian) Squadron
(October 1943/East Moor/No 6/QO)

No 463 (Australian) Squadron
(November 1943/Waddington/No 5/JO)

No 626 Squadron
(November 1943/Wickenby/No 1/UM)

No 576 Squadron
(November 1943/Elsham Wolds/No 1/UL)

No 630 Squadron
(December 1943/East Kirkby/No 5/LE)

No 622 Squadron
(December 1943/Mildenhall/No 3/GI)

No 15 Squadron
(December 1943/Mildenhall/ No 3/LS and DJ)

No 419 (Canadian) Squadron
(March 1944/Middleton St George/No 6/VR)

No 35 Squadron
(March 1944/Graveley/Nos 8 and 3/TL)

Opposite: **Merlin maintenance on a Lancaster during World War II.**

No 635 Squadron
(March 1944/Downham Market/No 8/F2)

No 75 (New Zealand) Squadron
(March 1944/Mepal/Nos 3 and 5/AA and JN)

No 582 Squadron
(April 1944/Little Staughton/No 8/6O)

No 300 (Polish) Squadron
(April 1944/Faldingworth/No 1/BH)

No 90 Squadron
(June 1944/Tuddenham/No 3/WP)

No 428 (Canadian) Squadron
(June 1944/Middleton St George/No 6/NA)

No 149 Squadron
(August 1944/Methwold/No 3/OJ)

No 218 Squadron
(September 1944/Methwold/No 3/HA)

No 195 Squadron
(October 1944/Witchford/No 3/A4 and JE)

No 186 Squadron
(October 1944/Tuddenham/No 3/XY and AP)

No 153 Squadron
(October 1944/Kirmington/No 1/P4)

No 227 Squadron
(October 1944/Bardney/No 5/9J)

No 170 Squadron
(October 1944/Kelstern/No 1/TC)

No 189 Squadron
(October 1944/Bardney/No 5/CA)

No 431 (Canadian) Squadron
(October 1944/Croft/No 6/SE)

No 150 Squadron
(November 1944/Fiskerton/No 5/IQ)

No 434 (Canadian) Squadron
(December 1944/Croft/No 6/IP and WL)

No 424 (Canadian) Squadron
(January 1945/Skipton-on-Swale/Nos 6 and 1/QB)

No 433 (Canadian) Squadron
(January 1945/Skipton-on-Swale/Nos 6 and 2/BM)

No 427 (Canadian) Squadron
(March 1945/Leeming/Nos 6 and 1/ZL)

No 138 Squadron
(March 1945/Tuddenham/No 3/NF and AC)

No 429 (Canadian) Squadron
(March 1945/Leeming/Nos 6 and 1/AL)

No 420 (Canadian) Squadron
(April 1945/Tholthorpe/No 6/PT)

Post-World War II
(first delivery/base)
by date of receipt of first aeroplane

No 425 (Canadian) Squadron
(May 1945/Tholthorpe)

Right: When the efforts of Bomber Command's Halifax and Lancaster bombers got fully into their stride, with electronic developments and the Pathfinder Force enhancing bombing accuracy, the British bombing offensive caused enormous damage to Germany's cities and the country's war economy.

No 279 (ASR) Squadron
(September 1945/Beccles)

No 104 Squadron
(November 1945/Abu Suwayr, Egypt)

No 178 Squadron
(November 1945/Fayid, Egypt)

No 214 Squadron
(November 1945/Fayid, Egypt)

No 40 Squadron
(January 1946/Ashallufah, Egypt)

No 179 (ASR) Squadron
(February 1946/St Eval)

No 37 Squadron
(April 1946/Fayid, Egypt)

No 70 Squadron
(April 1946/Fayid, Egypt)

No 621 (ASR) Squadron
(April 1946/Aqir, Palestine)

No 541 (PR) Squadron
(June 1946/Benson)

No 210 (MR) Squadron
(June 1946/St Eval)

No 38 (MR) Squadron
(July 1946/Luqa, Malta)

No 160 (GR) Squadron
(August 1946/Leuchars)

No 18 (GR) Squadron
(September 1946/En Shemer, Palestine)

No 82 (PR) Squadron
(October 1946/Benson)

No 224 (GR) Squadron
(October 1946/St Eval)

No 120 (GR) Squadron
(November 1946/Leuchars)

No 148 (B) Squadron
(November 1946/Upwood)

No 203 (MR) Squadron
(May 1947/St Eval)

No 683 (PR) Squadron
(November 1950/Fayid, Egypt)

The Lancaster also served with other units including:

Nos 1651, 1653, 1654, 1656, 1657, 1659, 1660, 1661, 1662, 1664, 1666, 1667, 1668 and 1669 Heavy Conversion Units

Nos 1678 and 1679 Heavy Conversion Flights

Nos 1, 3, 5 and 6 Lancaster Finishing Schools

No 6 OTU

Nos 230 and 236 Operational Conversion Units

No 1323 (Automatic Gun-Laying Training) Flight

No 1348 (Air/Sea Rescue) Flight

No 1384 Heavy Transport Flight

No 1577 (Special Duties) Flight

Nos 1 and 16 Ferry Units

Empire Test Pilots' School

Navigation Training Unit

Telecommunications Flying Unit

Torpedo Development Unit

Bombing Development Unit

Electronic Countermeasures Development Unit

Bomber Command Instructional School

Central Flying School

Central Gunnery School

Radio Warfare Establishment

Empire Air Armament School

RAF Flying College

Joint Anti-Submarine Warfare School

Index

Picture Credits

Hugh W. Cowin: 16 (b), 19, 21 (b), 22 (t), 23, 24, 28, 32, 34, 35 (b), 37 (both), 39, 45 (t), 68, 75, 83, 87 (both).
Philip Jarrett: 9 (both), 18 (b), 21 (t), 26, 31(b), 35 (t), 36, 38, 42 (both), 44, 49 (b), 51, 52, 53 (both), 57 (t), 59 (b), 60, 62, 63, 65, 66, 67, 69 (t), 70–71, 73, 77 (both), 80 (both), 81, 82, 86, 92, 93.

TRH Pictures: 6, 7, 8, 10, 11, 12, 13, 14, 15 (both), 16 (t), 17, 18 (t), 20, 22 (b), 25, 27, 29 (both), 30, 31 (t), 40, 41, 43, 45 (b), 46, 48, 49 (t), 50, 54, 55, 56, 57 (b), 58, 59, 64, 69 (b), 72, 74, 76, 78, 79, 88–89, 90–91.

Artworks: Aerospace Publishing